HOLLYWOOD'S FIRST CHOICES

HOLLYWOOD'S

FIRST CHOICES

(Or Why Groucho Marx Never Played Rhett Butler)

HOW THE GREATEST CASTING
DECISIONS WERE MADE

Jeff Burkhart & Bruce Stuart

Crown Trade Paperbacks
New York

A complete list of photograph
credits appears on page 223.

Copyright © 1994 by Jeff Burkhart and Bruce Stuart

Published by Crown Publishers, Inc., 201 East 50th Street, New York, New York
10022. Member of the Crown Publishing Group.

Random House, Inc. New York, Toronto, London, Sydney, Auckland
Crown Trade Paperbacks and colophon are trademarks of Crown Publishers, Inc.

Manufactured in the United States
Design by Debbie Glasserman

Library of Congress Cataloging-in-Publication Data
Burkhart, Jeff.
    Hollywood's first choices, or, Why Groucho Marx never played Rhett Butler) :
how Hollywood's greatest casting decisions were made / by Jeff Burkhart & Bruce
Stuart.—1st ed.
        p.   cm.
    Includes index.
    1. Motion pictures—United States—Casting.   2. Motion picture actors and
actresses—United States—Anecdotes.   I. Stuart, Bruce (Bruce Fullerton),
1950– .   II. Title.
PN1995.9.C34B87   1994
791.43′0233—dc20   93-25736
                                                                          CIP

ISBN 0-517-88086-5
10 9 8 7 6 5 4 3 2 1
First Edition

This book is affectionately
dedicated to Deborah Simon

ACKNOWLEDGMENTS

The authors of this book wish to thank the following people and companies who contributed to the creation of this book. They are: Our agent, Alan Nevins; our editor, Shaye Areheart, and her associate, Kelly Hammond; Gavin Lambert; Barry Sandler; Kaija Keel; David Baeder; David Hockney; Dyson Lovell; Todd Binkley; Cinema Collectors of Hollywood; Columbia Pictures; Sherry Lansing and Paramount Pictures; Turner Broadcasting; Universal Studios; Fred Zinnemann; Ron Pullen; David Landay; and Jean Howard.

Once again, thank you.

CONTENTS

x || Contents

"A Comeback Is Born"

With almost a hundred roles in a career spanning more than half a century, Bette Davis is today very much a Hollywood icon. Her unique New England personality coupled with a dynamic acting style secured for Miss Davis a well-deserved and popular reign as a Hollywood screen queen. She was a particularly potent commodity throughout the Depression-era thirties, winning two Best Actress Academy Awards in 1935 and 1938, respectively, by playing headstrong bad girls in *Dangerous* and *Jezebel*. Her popularity soared between 1939 and the end of World War II. She racked up an astounding five additional Best Actress nominations from the academy during this period for her riveting characterizations as the dying socialite in *Dark Victory*, the adulteress murderer of *The Letter*, the greedy Regina in Lillian Hellman's *The Little Foxes*, the vain, self-centered wife in *Mr. Skeffington*, and perhaps the most romantic Cinderella spinster ever in *Now, Voyager*. She was William Wyler's favorite actress, and he was considered perhaps the finest director of his time, responsible for such landmark films as *The Best Years of Our Lives* and *Wuthering Heights,* not to mention the three he made with Bette Davis.

Then, suddenly, everything started to collapse. The postwar years weren't at all kind to Bette Davis. After careening in a series of perilously overripe melodramas, her career hit rock bottom in the classic 1949 King Vidor stinker *Beyond the Forest,* an extraordinarily bad film made memorable today for being the role in which Miss Davis exclaims, "What a dump!" As the forties drew to a close, many of the power brokers in Hollywood felt Miss Davis's starring days were over as well. To revive her career would take nothing less than a miracle.

Meanwhile, if 1949 had proven a bleak year for Bette Davis, it was just the opposite for producer, director, and screenwriter Joseph L. Mankiewicz. He was well on his way to becoming the

A scheming Eve (Anne Baxter) has eyes for Margo Channing's (Bette Davis) boyfriend (Gary Merrill).

most respected film director in town. His credentials as a film producer included the wonderfully realized adaptation of *A Christmas Carol,* the hard-hitting social drama of Fritz Lang's *Fury,* and two of MGM's best sophisticated comedies, *The Philadelphia Story* and *Woman of the Year.* He began writing and directing after the war, creating the beautiful romance *The Ghost and Mrs. Muir* and the hit comedy-drama of 1949 *A Letter to Three Wives.* This stingingly witty exposé of married suburban women speculating on which of their husbands had run off with their best friend won Mankiewicz Academy Awards for Best Director and Best Screenplay. He chose to follow up his double-whammy delight with another story, once again focused on three different women, but this time in the world of the New York theater. Based on a short story by Mary Orr called ''The Wisdom of Eve,'' Mankiewicz turned a hard, savagely insightful eye on the problem women faced as they turned middle-aged and had to compete with younger, more attractive women, not only for their careers, but for their men as well. The screenplay was infused with some of the most dazzling dialogue ever heard on the screen. Its brilliance has not tarnished over the years. *All About Eve* is one of the best-written movies of all time.

Mankiewicz began casting *All About Eve* with 20th Century–Fox's studio chief, Darryl F. Zanuck, serving as producer. The role of the playwright's wife, best friend of legendary Broadway star Margo Channing—Karen Richards—was assigned to Celeste Holm, who had previously won a Best Supporting Actress Academy Award in Zanuck's *Gentleman's Agreement* and had also supplied the uncredited voice of Addie Ross, the unseen narrator of *A Letter to Three Wives.* Zanuck put pressure on a reluctant Mankiewicz to use another Fox player, Anne Baxter, for the title role of Eve Harrington, the relentless schemer of whom the film is all about. Baxter had also won a Best Supporting Actress award from the academy for still another Zanuck production, the 1946 version of W. Somerset Maugham's *The Razor's Edge.*

George Sanders was cast as the venomous theater critic Addison De Witt, a thinly disguised variation of legendary Broadway commentator Alexander Woolcott. Veteran scene stealer Thelma Ritter was set to play Margo Channing's dresser and confidante, and a young Marilyn Monroe made quite an impact in a very small role as Miss Caswell, a rather well-built but vacuous starlet on the make—a graduate of the "Copacabana School of Dramatic Arts."

The coveted role of Margo Channing was placed in the talented hands of Claudette Colbert, who had not only the radiance, but the rapier comic timing the role demanded. Colbert also had a vulnerable edge to her, a quality absolutely necessary to the inner workings of the character—an actress desperately afraid of growing old, alone and unloved.

Zanuck proclaimed *All About Eve* to be Fox's prestige film for 1950. According to Celeste Holm, who was later to be nominated for her performance as Karen Richards, the entire cast and crew knew from the very outset just how special this film would be. Mankiewicz rehearsed his cast for a month prior to

The sparkling cast of All About Eve. From left to right, Gary Merrill, Bette Davis, George Sanders, Anne Baxter, Hugh Marlowe, and Celeste Holm.

the actual start date. The first two weeks of shooting were set for early that spring in San Francisco at the Curran Theatre. It was imperative for the production to commence on schedule since the Curran was available only for those two weeks.

Everything was coming together beautifully until two weeks before the cameras were to roll. A disaster struck the production, a disaster that proved to be the very miracle Bette Davis so desperately needed for her comeback. Due to a back injury, Claudette Colbert was unable to work for at least six weeks. Since her character, Margo, was needed for virtually every sequence to be shot at the Curran, Mankiewicz and Zanuck were forced to recast their leading actress just ten days before production was to begin. In a moment of what proved to be inspired providence, Mankiewicz decided upon Bette Davis as his Margo Channing, over Zanuck's objections. Mankiewicz claims Davis arrived on the set for rehearsals the week before filming started and was letter perfect. She *was* Margo Channing. This was a great part, and Davis knew it. She was determined to make the most of it. And she did.

The film opened that October to rave reviews and sensational business. The critics praised the cast and screenplay, and Mankiewicz was now *the* premier writer-director working in Hollywood. But the most lavish reviews were over Bette Davis's triumphant comeback performance as Margo Channing. It was, and still is, her most magnificent creation. Once again Bette Davis was a force to be reckoned with. At the end of the year, Davis won the coveted New York Film Critics Award for Best Actress, as did the film for Best Picture of 1950. The following February *All About Eve* was nominated for a record fourteen Academy Award nominations, including one for Bette Davis as Best Actress and another for Anne Baxter in the same category. Thelma Ritter and Celeste Holm were nominated for Best Supporting Actress, and George Sanders was up for Best Supporting Actor. The Oscars that year presented incredibly stiff competi-

The original Margo Channing—Claudette Colbert.

tion in the Best Actress category. Davis was competing against not only Judy Holliday in *Born Yesterday,* but Gloria Swanson in her amazing comeback performance as the deranged silent-movie star Norma Desmond in Billy Wilder's superbly sardonic *Sunset Boulevard.* But the odds-on favorite was Bette Davis. *All About Eve* won six Academy Awards that year, including Best Picture and two to Mankiewicz for Best Writing and Best Direction, making him the only winner of both awards two years consecutively. George Sanders walked off with the Best Supporting Actor award, and Edith Head took the Best Costume award. But Bette Davis was overlooked; the Best Actress award went to Judy Holliday for her rich comic reprise of her Broadway hit as Billie Dawn in *Born Yesterday.*

Nevertheless, *All About Eve* was a strong enough comeback for Bette Davis to revive her career for the next five years. She was again nominated for Best Actress in 1952 for her role in *The Star* and was later to receive her tenth and final Academy Award nomination a decade later for her classic interpretation of Baby

The brilliance behind All About Eve, *Academy Award-winning writer and director Joseph L. Mankiewicz.*

Jane Hudson in the low-budget Gothic smash, *What Ever Happened to Baby Jane?*

Nearly forty years after the release of *All About Eve,* Bette Davis said that it was not only her favorite role, but the performance she would best like to be remembered for. Many critics and film buffs consider her Margo Channing one of the two or three greatest female performances ever recorded on film. And we, like Miss Davis, have only to thank Miss Colbert's bad back for making it all happen.

Since its inception, Hollywood has spawned dozens of films shamelessly exploiting its private fascination with its own peculiar landscape of madness. That curious state of mind known as Hollywood has often been the target of such talented directors as Preston Sturges in his Swiftian comedy *Sullivan's Travels,* Gene Kelly and Stanley Donen in their slaphappy musical, *Singin' in the Rain,* and Vincente Minnelli in his over-wrought *The Bad and the Beautiful.* But no one threw as lethal a punch at his own hometown as Billy Wilder did in his ghoulishly baroque black comedy *Sunset Boulevard.* Since its release in 1950, Hollywood has never been quite the same.

Billy Wilder, one of the world's consummate filmmakers, almost single-handedly elevated cynical one-liners into an art form, with his delicious mixture of jaded old-world sophistication shackled to a brash American audacity from which evolved "the vintage wisecrack." His amazing Hollywood career began by collaborating, most notably with the urbane Charles Brackett, on a successful string of late-thirties comedic screenplays.

One was *Ninotchka* with Greta Garbo and directed by Wilder's mentor, Ernst Lubitsch. Wilder bastardized *Snow White and the Seven Dwarfs,* resulting in Howard Hawks's superb screwball lark *Ball of Fire.* By 1942 Wilder was directing his own screenplays and broke through to the front ranks with the definitive film noir thriller *Double Indemnity,* followed by the Academy Award–winning Best Picture of 1945, *The Lost Weekend.* These films exhibited Wilder's genius of telling stories with deeply flawed or morally reprehensible characters whom he made recognizable and, ultimately, sympathetic to the moviegoing public. As the forties ended, Billy Wilder, *the* most celebrated writer/director on the Paramount lot, had Hollywood at his feet. Little did Hollywood know he was about to kick it down a long flight of stairs!

In 1948 Wilder was intrigued by Brackett's notion for a script depicting the tragic attempt at a modern-day film comeback by a wealthy but deranged famous ex–silent screen star, Norma Desmond, whose career was ruined by the advent of sound. With the help of Donald M. Marshman, Jr., Wilder and

Legendary silent screen director Erich von Stroheim played butler to silent screen star Gloria Swanson and leading man William Holden in Billy Wilder's Sunset Boulevard.

Brackett began their screenplay, fashioning a dark portrait of Hollywood, voicing their cynically accurate observations through the character Joe Guiness, a young, handsome, down-and-out screenwriter forced into prostituting himself as the mad ex–screen queen's kept lover. They used a murder mystery framework told in flashback by the corpse of the screenwriter, now floating in Norma Desmond's pool. They created a script with captivating characters, surprising plot twists, and some of the greatest dialogue ever spoken in any American film.

Recognizing the rich potential *Sunset Boulevard* offered, producer Charles Brackett and director Billy Wilder, with their considerable clout, were determined to cast their film with actors and actresses perfectly suited for the parts. Thus, with their best foot forward, they began searching for their Norma Desmond and fell flat on their faces.

Billy Wilder's first choice for his wildly unbalanced ex–screen queen was none other than the incomparable Mae West! By 1949 Mae West, her film career decidedly on the wane, had returned to the stage and become a successful nightclub entertainer. She was still enormously popular with the public, so one afternoon over lunch, Wilder courted her for his picture, elaborating to Miss West her part as the practically insane Norma Desmond. Her reaction was just short of violent. Highly insulted, she immediately turned Wilder down and, in the process, made perhaps the worst decision in her career.

Wilder and Brackett next solicited Mary Pickford, America's former sweetheart, but she too refused, finding both the character and story perverted and cruel. In retrospect one must be grateful for Pickford's decision, for although she might have made an interesting Norma Desmond, she wouldn't have been an explosive one. Another once popular silent screen star, Pola Negri, was approached, but she too said no. It seems that in some very basic way, the thought of portraying a washed-up old silent film star struck too deep a chord in these actresses. Per-

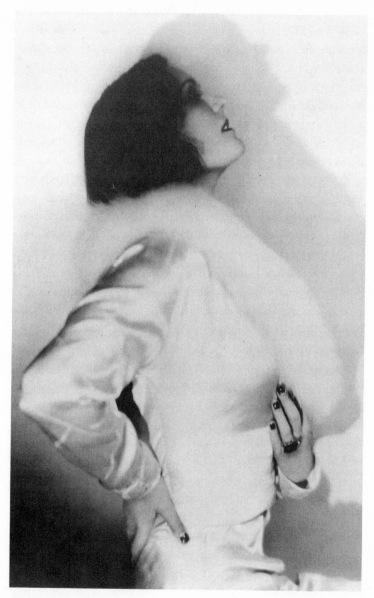

Pola Negri, one of Hollywood's leading silent screen stars, was sought by Wilder for the role of Norma Desmond.

haps they were afraid that the public might mistake their portrayal of the character as a reflection of their own personal lives. As sound had ruined Norma Desmond's career, it had had a somewhat similar impact on both Pickford's and Negri's screen careers. Pickford had wisely retired from acting in 1931 after winning an Academy Award for Best Actress two years before. But she felt uncomfortable in this new medium and thus quit as a highly respected and very wealthy member of the Hollywood community—town royalty, so to speak. Pola Negri had actually gone on to marry royalty after her screen career began to fade. Granted, when they'd stopped acting the parade hadn't yet passed them by, but it was just around the corner.

The now looming problem of casting the right actress for Norma Desmond was eventually solved by Wilder's friend and fellow director, the masterful George Cukor, acknowledged as the finest woman's director in the business. Cukor was knocked out after reading the script of *Sunset Boulevard*. He immediately recommended one of the silents' greatest stars, Gloria Swanson, for the part of Norma Desmond. Wilder was aware that it had been over twenty years since Swanson had made a film. She had gone on to a very lucrative stage career and was presently hosting "The Lux Theatre," a weekly dramatic radio anthology. Socially Swanson was held in esteem as a bright, beautiful woman who strongly advocated a diet of health foods and exercise. She could hardly be mistaken for a real-life Norma Desmond.

So they sent the script to Gloria Swanson. She read it at once and swiftly agreed to play the part. Miss Swanson's vanity wasn't about to stand in the way of playing a part *that* rich in a film directed by one of America's most brilliant directors.

It was, indeed, the smartest career move Miss Swanson ever made. It was for her thoroughly riveting performance as Norma Desmond that she will be best remembered, and at the time of the film's release, it was called one of the most astonishing comebacks Hollywood had ever witnessed. Swanson gave a silent screen performance, wildly exaggerated, fiery, and daring, using her face and body expressions to perfectly embody a once-great film star. She came dangerously close to being hammy, except Wilder and Brackett supplied her with some of the most cutting, scintillating dialogue any actress has had to deliver. When Norma Desmond tells Joe Guiness the silent screen idols didn't need sound—they had faces—Gloria Swanson made the audience believe and understand exactly what she meant.

Wilder, at first, had a much easier time casting the part of the down-and-out screenwriter turned gigolo. Paramount Pictures, the studio producing *Sunset Boulevard,* had recently signed Montgomery Clift to a handsome multipicture contract. At this time Clift was perhaps the hottest young screen actor in the world.

Before Brando or Dean or Newman, there was only Montgomery Clift, the most talked-about young screen actor of the postwar years. Ushering in the Method technique of acting, Clift represented a new breed of actor. He was the first naturalistic antihero, a man who could convincingly portray strength and vulnerability simultaneously. Championed by critics as an immensely gifted actor, he possessed tremendously compelling good looks that seduced young and old women alike, turning him into a sex symbol as well. Clift had worked for a number of years on Broadway in such plays as Thornton Wilder's *The Skin of Our Teeth* and *The Searching Wind* by Lillian Hellman, making quite a reputation for himself. He became an overnight sensation in his film debut opposite John Wayne in Howard Hawks's seminal western *Red River.* For his next film, Fred Zinnemann's *The Search,* Clift was nominated for an Academy Award as Best Actor, losing out to Ronald Colman in *A Double Life.* By 1949 he had just completed his first picture under his new Paramount contract, playing the scheming fortune hunter Morris Townsend in William Wyler's *The Heiress,* a splendid adaptation of Henry James's novel *Washington Square.* Wilder was anxious to secure Clift's participation in *Sunset Boulevard,* so he sent him the first fifty completed pages of the script to read. Based on only this portion, Clift agreed to play Joe Guiness. Brackett and Wilder were thrilled by this major casting coup. The news of Hollywood's most exciting young actor starring in Billy Wilder's latest production, *Sunset Boulevard,* hit papers across the country.

Preproduction began on *Sunset Boulevard.* One of the early pioneering giants of film, the notorious director and actor Erich von Stroheim, whose silent masterpieces *Foolish Wives, Greed,* and *The Wedding March* had profoundly influenced Wilder, was cast as Max, Norma Desmond's chauffeur. The ingenue role of Betty went to Nancy Olson, then the wife of Alan Jay Lerner, and director C. B. De Mille, who had indeed directed Miss Swanson in many of her best silent films, was cast to play none other than C. B. De Mille.

During this period, Montgomery Clift had left Los Angeles. In order to lead his private life, Clift had to stay out of Hollywood's hounding publicity limelight. For Clift was leading a double life, which included his homosexual preference, an ever-increasing dependency on prescription drugs and alcohol, and, at the time, his rather bizarre relationship with the infamous former torch song singer of the twenties Libby Holman, who years before had been tried for the shooting death of her young husband, the heir to the R. J. Reynolds tobacco fortune. Holman was acquitted, through family intervention, and inherited seven million dollars from the estate. Nearly thirty years Clift's senior, Holman flamed their affair by catering to Clift's every whim, including their shared indulgences with drugs. Holman tolerated Clift's homosexual involvements, but she was ruthlessly possessive of him in every other way. And he in turn became extremely dependent on her. After finishing *The Heiress* and before starting *Sunset Boulevard,* Clift left for Europe, where he stayed mostly in Switzerland. On his return home to Libby

Montgomery Clift backed out of Sunset Boulevard *ten days before shooting was to commence.*

Holman, he let her read the final script of *Sunset Boulevard.* When she realized Clift was about to play a kept lover to a wealthy woman twice his age, she became hysterical. For her, the story was too close for comfort. Holman gave Clift the following ultimatum: If he did *Sunset Boulevard,* she would commit suicide. Under these circumstances, Clift felt forced to call his agent and bow out of the production just weeks before it was to start shooting. Wilder was outraged by Clift's withdrawal, given the excuse that Clift felt he couldn't convincingly play a young man making love to a woman twice his age. It wasn't the kind of image he wanted to project. Wilder accepted Clift's excuse but thought it rather pathetic.

On April 11, 1949, just two weeks before the first day of shooting, Wilder and Brackett found themselves without a leading man. They quickly offered the role to Fred MacMurray, whose enormous success in Wilder's *Double Indemnity* had helped make him a superstar. MacMurray found Joe Guiness to be a morally repellent character and thus said no.

Wilder became desperate as the days flew by. Out of this desperation, the director submitted the script to a Paramount contract player, though he wasn't especially inspired by the idea of working with this actor. His name was William Holden.

William Holden had burst upon the screen ten years before as the unknown lead in the film version of Clifford Odets's *Golden Boy*. After that, Holden remained under contract to Paramount, first in juvenile roles and later as characters in second-rate B comedies. Holden was likable enough and was mildly popular with the moviegoing public, but he wasn't taken seriously as a dramatic actor. At first Holden felt uneasy about playing a kept man to an older has-been, even though he recognized the quality of the script. Under Wilder's insistence, the front office at Paramount applied pressure on Holden to agree to play Joe Guiness. Holden acquiesced and signed on just a week before the cameras were set to roll.

The cynical, opportunistic, and morally questionable part of Joe Guiness in *Sunset Boulevard* changed William Holden's life forever. He was nothing less than stunning. No one was prepared for the kind of ruthless, razor-tongued, and incredibly sexy performance Holden delivered. After *Sunset Boulevard* he was to become one of the most respected and popular actors of the fifties, with a career successfully spanning four decades. It was also the beginning of a strong friendship between Holden and Wilder, who were to work together on several more movies.

Sunset Boulevard was a critical success when released in the summer of 1950. The academy nominated the film for Best Picture, Holden for Best Actor, Swanson for Best Actress, Nancy Olson for Best Supporting Actress, and Erich von Stroheim for Best Supporting Actor. The direction, the screenplay, and a number of technical achievements were graced with nominations as well. Holden was the heavy odds-on favorite to win for Best Actor, but he lost to José Ferrer for his performance in *Cyrano de Bergerac*. People were outraged by Holden's defeat. In fact, *Sunset Boulevard* lost to Fox's *All About Eve* in almost every major category, except for Original Screenplay. Many felt the academy's slight toward *Sunset Boulevard* was the result of the film's unrelentingly harsh attitude toward Hollywood. But in reality it just became runner-up to another classic film—*All About Eve*.

Sunset Boulevard was to be the final collaboration between Charles Brackett and Billy Wilder. Their magical union ended bitterly, with neither party claiming to know the reason for the split.

Three years later, in 1953, Montgomery Clift was nominated for his third Academy Award as Best Actor in the biggest film of the year, *From Here to Eternity*. Clift was certain he would take home the gold statue, but he lost to William Holden in the Billy Wilder–directed screen version of the Broadway play *Stalag 17*. Holden remained forever grateful to Wilder for giving him a chance to make good in a role that forged Holden's screen persona for the rest of his career.

The premier American film director of the thirties was, undoubtedly, Frank Capra. Beginning with *It Happened One Night,* Capra was three times honored with Academy Awards as Best Director, in 1934, 1936, and 1938. His films, especially the comedies, were unique and snappy blends of old-fashioned populist American sentiment with screwball antics and behavior. Capra's hits turned Columbia Pictures into a major studio on a par with Paramount and Metro-Goldwyn-Mayer.

His three most lucrative achievements were *You Can't Take It with You, Mr. Deeds Goes to Town,* and *Mr. Smith Goes to Washington.* The latter two films greatly affected the respective screen careers of Gary Cooper and James Stewart, as well as that of the ever-remarkable Jean Arthur, their costar in both films, who by the decade's end was Frank Capra's leading lady. Although lacking the recognition of a Garbo or Dietrich, Arthur, with a career spanning through the thirties up till her last screen performance in the 1953 western classic *Shane,* was adored by audiences, who closely identified with the characters she created through her sublime comic timing and a pixilated speaking voice. Besides the Capra hits, Jean Arthur enjoyed many successes in such memorable vehicles as Howard Hawks's *Only Angels Have Wings* and George Stevens's *The More the Merrier*.

On screen Jean Arthur was, without question, nothing short of magical. Off screen, though, particularly during filming, she was more a full-scale horror show. Even under the guidance of De Mille, Ford, or Wyler, Arthur was often plagued by a paralyzing insecurity, making her difficult at best. Matters weren't helped by her cold, offputting personality and her reluctance to fraternize with the rest of the cast and crew. Yet even the thorniest director would rattle through with Jean, knowing she'd deliver the goods somehow. Yet as the post–World War II era began, Jean Arthur found herself—like Capra—no longer at the top of the Hollywood heap. She hadn't had anything remotely like a hit in over two years. Worse, there were no interesting film prospects in the offering. So, like so many before her, Jean Arthur decided to star on Broadway.

For her return engagement, Arthur selected a new political comedy by a former RKO boy wonder named Garson Kanin. Kanin had developed a play set in the corrupt world of Washington politics, where an unlikely Pygmalion story unfolds. His inspired central character, Billie Dawn, an amazingly dumb blonde who's the browbeaten mistress of a shifty but powerful junkyard tycoon, was brilliantly conceived and just the tonic Arthur's career needed. For the role of Harry Brock, the junkyard king, Kanin had used for inspiration Harry Cohn, the tyrannical boss of Columbia Pictures, investing the racketeer Brock with many of Cohn's unethical personality traits. Paul Douglas was cast as Harry. The entire venture was announced and scheduled for the 1946 Broadway season under the title *Born Yesterday*. With its lofty credentials, *Born Yesterday* became one of the most eagerly anticipated events of the coming season. Oddly enough, Kanin hired a relatively unknown revue star as Jean Arthur's understudy, feeling, perhaps, that the vivacious twenty-four-year-old would not be seen as a potential threat to the show's possibly temperamental star. The revue star had come highly recommended to Kanin by no less than Betty Comden, Jerome Robbins, Adolph Green, and Leonard Bernstein, impressive references for an understudy. Kanin admits seeing something special in the actress on their first meeting, but he failed to explore further once rehearsals began. The understudy's real name was Judith Tuvim. Her stage name was Judy Holliday.

Rehearsals for *Born Yesterday*'s out-of-town opening initially proved promising, although Arthur was already complaining over her difficulty in memorizing so large a part. Director Kanin marveled at her absolute comedic grasp of Billie Dawn and was no less impressed by Paul Douglas and, in fact, the entire cast. (Miss Arthur's understudy run-through transpired before the stage manager instead of Mr. Kanin himself.)

The out-of-town opening confirmed that both Jean Arthur and the play were terrific. Everyone thought so, except, that is, for Miss Arthur, who felt both she and the play stank! Nothing Kanin said or did could convince the now terrified Arthur of her misconceptions. Ultimately it was a losing battle, for Miss Arthur's private demons proved to be powerful adversaries. Just prior to the scheduled Broadway opening, Jean Arthur quit the show, citing health reasons for her departure to the press. At eight-thirty that evening, much to Kanin's distress and consternation, the understudy went on as Billie Dawn for an audience already disappointed at not seeing a real live movie star. Two and a half hours later the curtain fell on a theatrical miracle. As the former chorus girl and dumb blonde par excellence, Judy Holliday gave a legendary performance.

On February 4, 1946, a stunning array of New York society gathered at the Lyceum Theatre to attend the Broadway debut of *Born Yesterday*. Among them was Kanin's dear friend Katharine Hepburn, who was anxious to see this young understudy

Kanin had been raving to her about. Once again Holliday delivered a howlingly funny and yet utterly compassionate performance that completely awed the first-night audience and critics alike. No greater convert was won that night than Katharine Hepburn, who immediately began championing Holliday to anyone who would listen. Suddenly Judy Holliday had arrived. She stayed with the show for two years, virtually selling out all performances. Her face graced the covers of *Time* and *Life* magazines, where she was hailed as a new theatrical comet.

As Judy settled in for a long run, Garson Kanin began sifting through the various film offers for *Born Yesterday* while he and his wife, actress Ruth Gordon, wrote an original screenplay to star Katharine Hepburn and Spencer Tracy, a spirited courtroom battle of the sexes nimbly titled *Adam's Rib*. Naturally Kanin, like everyone else, assumed the screen adaptation of *Born Yesterday* would allow Judy Holliday to re-create her stage triumph. Ironically, the highest offer—that of one million dollars—came from none other than Harry Cohn for Columbia Pictures. With bemusement, Kanin quickly accepted the deal. Several weeks later Cohn officially announced Columbia's acquisition of *Born Yesterday* at one of the highest prices ever paid for a straight play. He also made known his intention of using his most valuable female star under contract at Columbia: Miss Rita Hayworth! This news stunned Judy Holliday, but she had no grounds to wage a campaign for the part. She had only appeared once before on screen, in George Cukor's 1944 film *Winged Victory,* a performance that slipped by without causing much attention. Harry Cohn frankly did not like Judy Holliday, referring to her as "that fat Jewish broad." He'd be damned if he would put her in a film that had already cost him and the studio a million dollars. Cohn refused to see a screen test Holliday had made. He wanted a star, and if it wasn't going to be Hayworth, it would be Barbara Stanwyck or Lucille Ball. Cohn's decision enraged Katharine Hepburn, who, along with Spencer Tracy and George

Cukor, determined to make certain that Judy Holliday played Billie Dawn in Harry Cohn's screen version of *Born Yesterday.*

George Cukor, one of Hollywood's finest and most prolific directors, was Cohn's choice for *Born Yesterday.* Cukor quickly accepted the assignment, although privately he groused at the idea of not having Holliday for the film. But before *Born Yesterday* could begin shooting, Cukor had to fulfill another commitment to film Tracy and Hepburn in the M-G-M production of the Kanins' *Adam's Rib.* Cukor thus decided to cast Judy Holliday in an important secondary role in *Adam's Rib,* a choice thoroughly blessed by his two costars. These three conspirators—Tracy, Hepburn, and Cukor—decided the only way to convince Cohn on Holliday for *Born Yesterday* was by showcasing her prodigious talents in their current film, playing the part of Doris Attinger, a dumb blond second cousin of Billie Dawn's.

Filming on *Adam's Rib* began in May of 1949 in New York City. Holliday filmed by day while playing Billie on stage at night. Finding herself working alongside such luminaries as Tracy and Hepburn overwhelmed Holliday. She was often unnerved on the set (which happily contributed enormously to her performance), so Katharine Hepburn and George Cukor went out of their way to work with Holliday. Hepburn became Holliday's patron saint and mentor, guiding her through the film as much as Cukor. In their first important scene together—a nine-minute dialogue sequence between attorney and client—Hepburn allowed the camera to linger almost solely on Holliday, a generous gesture rarely shown by an established star to a newcomer. The magic known as Judy Holliday was coming through on film, and Cukor was delighted with the results (oddly enough, like Miss Arthur before her, Miss Holliday was convinced she was incompetent in her role). As *Born Yesterday* was closing its Broadway run at the very end of 1949—New Year's Eve, to be exact—M-G-M was releasing its Christmas gift,

Adam's Rib. The movie was an immediate hit, both critically and financially, and Miss Holliday, in her supporting role, was hailed as the screen discovery of the year. It was finally, at this point, that Cohn acquiesced and cast Judy Holliday as Billie Dawn. The trick had succeeded: the conspirators had conspired' victoriously.

By the time filming on *Born Yesterday* began, Miss Holliday had shed fifteen pounds. Broderick Crawford, fresh from winning an Oscar as Best Actor of 1949 in Columbia's searing adaptation of Robert Penn Warren's *All the King's Men,* accepted the role of Harry Brock after Paul Douglas—who was enjoying a film career of his own—turned it down. William Holden, a competent but second-string contract player at the time, was cast as the young journalist. Before the year was out, Holden would forever change his image with his maverick performance in Billy Wilder's classic *Sunset Boulevard.* Under Cukor's fluid, seamless direction and a first-rate but uncredited screen adaptation by Kanin himself, *Born Yesterday* was even better on film than on stage. Cukor managed to tone down Holliday's theatrics and lost nothing in doing so. Her comedy timing was wondrous to behold. And this opinion was echoed by the critics and moviegoing public when the film was released as Columbia's Christmas package for 1950.

Born Yesterday was nominated for Best Picture, Best Actress, and Best Direction, among others, by the Academy of Motion Picture Arts and Sciences. Miss Holliday's competition was especially stiff, perhaps the toughest ever; also vying for the award were the sensational comeback performances of Bette Davis in *All About Eve* and Gloria Swanson in *Sunset Boulevard.* Miss Davis, after winning the New York Film Critics Award and the Golden Globe for Best Actress, was the odds-on favorite. Come Oscar night, Judy Holliday, seated next to George Cukor, found herself the winner as the Best Actress of 1950 for *Born Yesterday.* After the ceremony, a jubilant Judy Holliday rushed next door to a Chinese restaurant, along with Cukor, to telephone her mother back in New York with news of her victory.

Judy Holliday and George Cukor made two more films together, *The Marrying Kind* (1952) and *It Should Happen to You* (1954), both scripted by Garson Kanin. Neither was equal to *Born Yesterday*. In 1956 Holliday returned to Broadway in the musical smash *Bells Are Ringing,* for which performance she won a Tony Award. Holliday repeated the role in the 1960 screen version directed by Vincente Minnelli, but it lacked the heights reached on Broadway. Unfortunately, Judy Holliday died in 1964 at the age of forty-three from cancer, cutting a brilliant career very short indeed. But for as long as she was around, Holliday was beloved as someone unique and wonderful and, in large part because of her screen performance in *Born Yesterday,* is cherished by audiences today. And, to a very real degree, we have Katharine Hepburn, Spencer Tracy, and George Cukor to thank for that.

QUEEN CHRISTINA

(1934)

Just as the politically turbulent thirties began, Sir Noël Coward, the bona fide theater genius of London's West End, found himself enjoying his greatest triumph to date in his gossamer masterpiece *Private Lives,* a moral duel of sexual wit that set a standard of sophistication that virtually defined an entire decade. Written letter perfect in just three days on a luxury liner in the South Seas, the original London and subsequent New York productions were directed by and starred Coward. He conceived the role of Amanda for his gloriously frequent costar, Gertrude Lawrence. They were, quite simply, perfect. Yet, retrospectively, these original productions of *Private Lives* are sometimes best remembered as the place where a relatively little-known young British actor was transformed into an enormous matinee idol, in the supporting role of Amanda's second husband, Victor. Among London theater circles, the youthful actor was thought of as still another of Mr. Coward's "protégés," which, for many, was viewed as a questionable distinction, taking into account Sir Noël's sexual proclivities.

Nevertheless, in 1930 there was no doubt that the remarkably handsome young Laurence Olivier was experiencing, for the very first time, the perfumed intoxication that only a smash hit comedy could so easily exude.

Olivier's newly found matinee idol status secured parts for him in several early British talkies, but his utter contempt for the new medium was arrogantly displayed in his hammy acting performances. Still, Olivier's popularity grew in England, no doubt enhanced by his marriage to actress Jill Esmond, who at the time was a much better-known stage personality than her husband. (Ms. Esmond would eventually leave both her husband and virtually her career for the arms of another *woman*.) When *Private Lives* arrived in New York, Miss Esmond was now a part of the cast in the role of Sybil. It was during the course of this run that the Oliviers caught the attention of Hollywood studio executives who were, at this time, raiding the legitimate stage for actors and actresses who could speak well—this being the age of the "talkies." Metro-Goldwyn-Mayer expressed interest in Olivier, while RKO, under the young and tenacious

Greta Garbo and her former lover John Gilbert starred in Queen Christina. *It was the last of their many pairings.*

leadership of David O. Selznick, was anxious to secure Miss Esmond's talents. Thus, upon the conclusion of their contractual obligations to *Private Lives,* the Oliviers headed west for Los Angeles, riding feverishly high on the hopes of being Hollywood film stars. They stayed for nearly two years, long enough to have their hopes kicked out of them.

Olivier floundered uneventfully in three costume pictures, all forgettable, while Selznick kept after his wife to sign a seven-year exclusive contract, dangling the coveted lead in *A Bill of Divorcement* as an enticement. Eventually Olivier stopped his wife from signing with Selznick when he learned that the producer intended to use another actress for the part Ms. Esmond so eagerly sought. (The part was played by newcomer Katharine Hepburn; it was her first screen appearance and instantly established her as a star.) For years after, Selznick blamed Olivier for ruining Esmond's career by insisting that she return to England with him in 1932. In fact, Selznick initially didn't care much for Olivier, whom he found flighty and conceited, a young lad desperately in need of being slapped down to size. What Selznick didn't know at the time was that Olivier would soon get his much deserved slap, and from the hand of Hollywood's greatest actress, the magnificent Greta Garbo. Her slap sent Olivier back to England. It would be seven years before the century's greatest actor would return to Hollywood.

As the twentieth century rapidly nears its end, it would be an accurate assessment to say that Greta Garbo, along with Marilyn Monroe, is the most famous screen actress ever to be created by the Hollywood studio system. In the annals of film history, there have been better actresses than Garbo and a few as beautiful, but, like Monroe, no one has been as adored by the camera as Garbo. Perhaps it was her radiant skin, her constantly emoting eyes, and the veiled mystique she so adroitly generated that made her riveting on screen. Her every little gesture was compelling. She was just extraordinary, the essence of a film star, and a legend till the day she died. The public's fascination for Garbo never wavered even fifty years after she had made her last motion picture and retired from public view.

A silent Swedish film, *The Story of Gösta Berling* (1923), directed by Mauritz Stiller and starring his fresh young creation, Miss Greta Garbo, captured the attention of Louis B. Mayer, the mastermind of the newly formed Metro-Goldwyn-Mayer film studio. Mayer imported both of them. And although Stiller did work in Hollywood, most notably on *The Wind* with Lillian Gish, he eventually returned to Sweden, soured by the entire studio system experience. On the other hand, under Mayer's careful exploitation, Garbo flourished, embarking on a strikingly successful silent screen career. Mayer teamed Garbo with the very handsome John Gilbert, the star of M-G-M's megablockbuster, King Vidor's 1925 war classic *The Big Parade*. The couple appeared in a series of silent love stories, including *Romance* and the erotically charged *Flesh and the Devil,* catapulting them into stardom as the screen's most popular acting couple of the silent era. Then along came *The Jazz Singer,* and within two years sound reigned in Hollywood. Many acting careers were destroyed, unable to make the transition to talkies. One of those who found great difficulty in this period was, in fact, M-G-M's ultimate silent screen actor, John Gilbert. His voice was undeniably thin and high-pitched. Worse still was his acting. He seemed fey rather than virile, affected instead of affecting. Nevertheless, Gilbert remained in the public's good graces through news of his and Garbo's off-screen love affair, fed continually to the press by Mayer's zealous publicity department. All of this culminated in a lavish wedding ceremony for Garbo and Gilbert, paid for by Louis B. Mayer himself. But Garbo literally left Gilbert high and dry at the altar by failing to show up. Later that day, when Mayer suggested to a frantic Gilbert that he just sleep with Garbo and forget marrying her, Gilbert responded by punching Louis B. Mayer in the mouth. That sock to the jaw marked the beginning of the end not only for John Gilbert's career, but for his very life. Louis B. Mayer never forgot or forgave Gilbert for the insult.

More important, as far as Mayer and the M-G-M stockholders were concerned, was Garbo's career. She was the more prized asset. And when Garbo finally did talk in Clarence Brown's screen adaptation of Eugene O'Neill's Pulitzer Prize—winning play *Anna Christie* (1930), the moviegoing public around the world stopped and listened to every word she spoke. The voice perfectly matched the image; just as Garbo had conquered silent films, so did she triumph in talkies. Over the next three years Garbo made a string of hit films for M-G-M, including the Oscar-winning *Grand Hotel* (1932) and the campy but successful *Mata Hari*. Her salary soared, and so did her demands as she sought to attain as much autonomy from Mayer's iron-fisted control as humanly possible. She also shunned any kind of publicity, wishing "to be alone." And as long as Garbo's pictures continued to make money, Mayer was content to stay away from her and generally approve the films she wished to star in with the director and leading men of her own choosing.

In 1932 Garbo managed to persuade Mayer to produce one of her pet projects, a lavish, epic costume drama called *Queen Christina*. It was an unquestionable vanity star vehicle, in which Garbo was to portray the notorious seventeenth-century monarch who ultimately abdicated the Swedish throne, in this version for the man she loves. One of Paramount's top directors, the stylish and innovative Reuben Mamoulian, was imported to M-G-M on Garbo's urging. Her favorite writer and confidante Salka Viertel and the prestigious New York playwright Sam Behrman took on the job of writing the script. Mayer ran into trouble, though, when he began casting about for Garbo's leading man. The top stars under the M-G-M banner were wary of appearing in a Garbo vehicle. Garbo had suggested her former costar John Gilbert, who was desperate for work, but Mayer

The magnificent Garbo grieves as Sweden's queen.

fought her on this point. Instead he somehow managed to convince a very apprehensive Garbo into accepting a young British actor whom Walter Wanger, the film's official line producer, had suggested after remembering him from the New York production of *Private Lives*. Garbo let it be known she was extremely unimpressed by Olivier's Hollywood film credentials, three justifiably forgotten films, but Mamoulian was keen on using Olivier as well. Thus Garbo consented to Laurence Olivier as her new leading man in *Queen Christina*.

Laurence Olivier arrived on the M-G-M lot to start production on *Queen Christina* just filled with himself. After all, his leading lady was the most famous movie star in the world. Their first meeting was made memorable only by how unimpressed Garbo seemed to be with Olivier. From the very outset she built a wall between them, and things became worse once shooting began. It became apparent to all involved, including the young leading man, that Laurence Olivier was hopelessly out of his league acting with Greta Garbo. After the first week of shooting, Garbo stopped speaking to Olivier off the set. He tried to win her over one afternoon, but she told him all his small talk was "very painful to listen to." By the end of the second week of shooting, Garbo began to lay down the law. She insisted Olivier be fired and John Gilbert be hired to replace him immediately; otherwise she would quit the film. With an expensive production such as *Queen Christina,* and with two weeks of shooting already completed, Mayer was forced to submit to Garbo's demands. Walter Wanger thus paid off Olivier, saying how much he admired the young actor and was convinced he would eventually have a successful film career. Olivier and his wife used part of the settlement money to take a holiday in Hawaii. Afterward they returned to England, where, over the next seven years, Olivier became England's greatest stage actor, second only to Sir John Gielgud, and

Jill Esmond would become one of England's most celebrated lesbians.

John Gilbert costarred in *Queen Christina,* unmemorably. It was his last hurrah, and its failure, as well as his terrible notices, forever destroyed his once-brilliant screen career. The film was not particularly embraced by either the public or the critics, but Garbo's performance was considered a masterpiece. The last moment of the film, a glorious close-up of Garbo on the boat carrying her away from Sweden, is a one-of-a-kind tour de force that elicits applause from the viewing audiences. It's *the* ultimate star close-up with the ultimate movie star face. It's an unforgettable moment.

Garbo's career sailed along smoothly throughout the thirties, though her box office returns were diminishing noticeably. She gave classic performances in *Camille, Anna Karenina,* and *Ninotchka,* but after a 1941 modern sex comedy, *Two-Faced Woman,* a total fiasco from start to finish, Garbo abruptly retired at the age of thirty-six. She never made another film and lived a reclusive life, mostly in New York City. She never married. And she considered *Queen Christina* to be her finest film.

In 1936 John Gilbert died of a massive heart attack at the age of thirty-seven. Those who knew him said he'd died of a disillusioned life. The public had nearly forgotten him at the time of his death. Today he's best remembered for *The Big Parade* and his silent films with Garbo, but he's not considered to be a fine actor—rather a better movie star.

Laurence Olivier did return to Hollywood some years after *Queen Christina* to play Heathcliff in William Wyler's romantic film version of Emily Brontë's *Wuthering Heights.* It would make Olivier an international film star, a position he firmly held on to till his death at the age of eighty-eight. His marriage to Vivien Leigh was one of the great romances of the twentieth century, or so it was in the public's mind. He was knighted in 1948 and won an Academy Award for his title performance in *Hamlet* the same year. He was later made a lord. Upon his death he was acknowledged throughout the world as the greatest English-speaking actor of the century. As for Miss Garbo, Olivier claimed never to have met her again after 1933.

Since the inception of producing commercial film productions, the biography, or "bio," film genre has flourished. Sarah Bernhardt's only screen performance was in a 1913 silent movie where she played Queen Elizabeth I, rather floridly, too. The French filmmaker Abel Gance astonished the world in 1926 with his masterwork, *Napoleon,* a four-and-a-half-hour epic that is perhaps the greatest silent film ever made. Its technical innovations still appear revolutionary, even by today's standards. During the thirties Hollywood produced a slew of bios, most notably by Warner Brothers, starring the imaginative actor's actor Paul Muni. The public clamored for the screen bios, which they found educating in a highly entertaining and painless fashion, although Hollywood's rendition of history often had nothing to do with the real thing. And the screen bio proved a tremendous stage for an actor to fuse his talents and energies with a bigger-than-life *real* character. Actors and actresses could pull out all the stops and wow their audiences with their impersonations. And in no other genre is casting as important as finding the perfect actor to play the title character. The film ultimately is made or broken by this performance, so it's crucial that it be right on target. In the thirties alone, the Oscar was awarded to George Arliss as Disraeli, Charles Laughton as Henry VIII, Paul Muni as Louis Pasteur, Luise Rainer as Anna Held, Joseph Schildkraut as Captain Dreyfus, Alice Brady as Mrs. O'Leary, and Spencer Tracy as Father Flanagan of Boys Town. *The Great Ziegfeld* and *The Life of Emile Zola* won for Best Picture of 1936 and 1937, respectively. And this tradition would continue on into today's films, with Ben Kingsley as Gandhi, George C. Scott as Patton, and Jeremy Irons as Claus von Bülow. Perhaps screen biographies reached an apex in the sixties with two performances in particular—Barbra Streisand's Fanny Brice in *Funny Girl* and Peter O'Toole's monumental portrayal of Colonel T. E. Lawrence, better known throughout the world as Lawrence of Arabia.

Peter O'Toole was introduced to international film audiences in this 1962 production, and his impact was immediate— something extraordinary and shattering, mythic in size and dimension. Granted, *Lawrence of Arabia,* even without O'Toole, would be recognized as a masterpiece of inspired direction and photography, but *with* O'Toole's soaring performance, *Lawrence* is the finest epic screen biography of our times.

No one could have played it better than Peter O'Toole, but he was hardly the first choice and nearly didn't play the role at all.

Young Peter O'Toole, the fiery Irish actor, was swiftly making a formidable reputation, both on and off stage, as the "angry young men of the British theater" were emerging in the late fifties and early sixties. His Shakespearean performances at the then fledgling Royal Shakespeare Company, under the direction of Sir Peter Hall, had won him critical and public acclaim, as had his appearance in *The Long and the Short and the Tall* at London's Royal Court Theatre. He was set to play Henry II in Jean

Marlon Brando was director David Lean's original choice for Lawrence of Arabia.

Anouilh's new historical drama *Becket*. Off stage O'Toole was notorious as the biggest drunk since Richard Burton, and although he was married to the very talented actress Sian Phillips, he was perfecting womanizing as an art form all its own. His only major attempt to break into films was an absolutely disastrous screen test he had made for the part of Dr. Sugar in the screen transference of Tennessee Williams's Gothic one-act, *Suddenly, Last Summer*. The test was so frightful that it was quickly dismissed by the film's director, Joseph L. Mankiewicz, and its producer, the flamboyant but audacious Sam Spiegel.

At that time, Sam Spiegel was fresh from another major triumph, his epic adventure production *The Bridge on the River Kwai*. The film, a prisoner-of-war story set in Ceylon and based

Unknown to the Western world, Egyptian actor Omar Sharif became an international star in Lawrence of Arabia.

on actual fact, was directed by England's finest director, David Lean, and it was easily Lean's best work to date. The film won seven Academy Awards, including one for Best Picture, one for Best Actor (Alec Guinness, who was shortly thereafter knighted by the queen), and one for Best Director.

Kwai worked on many levels. It was not only a marvelous action adventure film with exotic locales and unbearable suspense; it was also a character study of surprising insight and an indictment of war, particularly its insidious power to brainwash even the most moral of men into doing deeds of utter madness and treason. Alec Guinness, as the mad Colonel Nicholson, was magnificent, subtle, and methodical. The actor and the director had fought bitterly during the film over the interpretation, but Lean won out, and so did the film. But their arguments preceded the shooting of the movie, when Guinness had learned from Lean that he'd not been first choice for the part of Colonel Nicholson—that he was, in fact, a replacement for both Noël Coward, who had turned it down, and Charles Laughton, who had become too ill to play the part. Guinness bitterly resented this, although Lean later denied the story completely. On top of all this, the theme song from the film, "Colonel Bogie's Theme," became the number one–selling record throughout the world. Everything about *Kwai* was terrific, and Spiegel was more than anxious to reteam with Lean. But on what? Spiegel wasn't to worry. After all, he had produced *The African Queen* and *On the Waterfront* prior to *Kwai*. He might be gruff in person, but he had a shrewd eye for a good story.

At this particular juncture in time, David Lean was right at the forefront of filmmaking. His agility at conveying a narrative through images cleverly edited in a distinct context had justly earned him the reputation of a master storyteller, evolving no doubt from his strong affection for English literary traditions such as Dickens and E. M. Forster, among others. His skill with actors was immense. And his sense of the visuals was at worst handsome and at best dead-on right and beautiful. An artist genuinely in love with film, David Lean began as an apprentice tea server at a studio in London during the silent days of the British film industry. Eventually he became England's foremost film editor, creatively cutting *Pygmalion* for Anthony Asquith and *The Forty-ninth Parallel* for Michael Powell. His directorial breakthrough came about as the result of another master not really caring about directing a film he was about to direct. The master was Sir Noël Coward, who had decided his "war effort" would be a film he would write, produce, star in, and direct. The film, entitled *In Which We Serve,* would be about a captain and his ship and crew during the early days of World War II. Coward was delighted by the entire enterprise, except for one drawback: he had never directed a movie. Of course he could get performances, set the mood and tone, just as he had done countless times for his own stage productions, but the technical end of filmmaking not only baffled him, it bored him to tears. So Coward decided to hire an assistant, so to speak, who'd handle the technical end of directing, and he would concentrate on the actors. The man Coward hired was David Lean. They got on famously. After two weeks of shooting, Coward realized how talented and sensitive Lean was, not only with the visuals, but with the acting company. By the end of the third week Lean had been given full control of the production while Coward essentially remained the actor/author of the piece.

In Which We Serve proved to be the most splendid war film made by Great Britain and was hailed as a masterpiece. It was nominated for an Academy Award for Best Picture, and Noël Coward was awarded a special statue for his contributions to the film. Thus began a collaboration between Coward and Lean that

Veteran character actor Anthony Quinn played against the relatively unknown Peter O'Toole who replaced Albert Finney in the title role.

ended with *Brief Encounter* (1946), one of the best-loved romances ever put on screen. Lean followed this with his extraordinary Dickens adaptations of *Great Expectations* and *Oliver Twist,* arguably the two finest examples of Dickens on film. Now, with *The Bridge on the River Kwai,* Lean had made a superior widescreen epic of weight and importance. He had continually topped himself throughout his career. How could he top *Kwai?*

Lean turned down an offer to direct Kirk Douglas's slave epic, *Spartacus,* and began concentrating on a film biography of Gandhi, hiring Emeric Pressburger to write the script. Gandhi fascinated Lean as a man revered by the world, but whose private life was fraught with demons and egomania. Also, Lean desperately wanted to film once more in unusual landscapes, particularly India. But eventually Lean's deep concerns of oversimplifying and thereby trivializing India's great liberator by dramatizing his life in three hours forced him to abandon the project. Twenty years later, Sir Richard Attenborough's sanctimonious film on Gandhi justified all of Lean's suspicions. In the meantime, the great David Lean was without a project on hand.

Enter Sam Spiegel with an offer for David Lean to direct an epic based on *The Seven Pillars of Wisdom,* T. E. Lawrence's massive memoirs of his desert campaign waged against the Turks during World War I. Spiegel's coup was in obtaining the film rights to the memoirs from Lawrence's family. The notion of filming the story of Lawrence of Arabia was certainly not a novel one. Alexander Korda had announced a production to star Leslie Howard before World War II, but with the advent of war, Churchill felt it was important to retain Turkey as an ally and dissuaded Korda from the project. In 1958 another film version, based on a biography by Anthony Nutting, was announced by director Anthony Asquith, with a screenplay by the highly regarded playwright Terence Rattigan, to star Dirk Bogarde in the title role. But this version was shelved when Sam Spiegel and

David Lean announced their production of *The Seven Pillars of Wisdom*, later known as *Lawrence of Arabia*. Rattigan cleverly rewrote his film script as a stage vehicle called *Ross*, which was received successfully in London with Alec Guinness as Lawrence and in New York with John Mills in the title role.

The first casting bombshell landed in late 1959 when Sam Spiegel informed the press that Marlon Brando was going to play Lawrence of Arabia. Spiegel and Brando had worked together on *On the Waterfront*, and Lean regarded Brando as the greatest actor of all time. But casting Brando as T. E. Lawrence would have been equivalent to having Marilyn Monroe play Queen Victoria. The announcement caused public outrage in the British press. How could an American possibly play the British liberator of Damascus? Fortunately Brando had to back down, since he was too involved with the remake of *Mutiny on the Bounty*, where his performance as the somewhat fey and foppish Fletcher Christian (radically different from Clark Gable's interpretation) gives us some indication of how Brando might have portrayed Lawrence. Interesting, perhaps, but ultimately wrong. Next came announcements for the supporting cast. Cary Grant was to play General Allenby, Jack Hawkins Colonel Newcombe, Horst Buchholz Sheik Ali, and Sir Laurence Olivier Prince Feisal. The only actor to actually appear in the film was Jack Hawkins, in the role of General Allenby. Meanwhile the script originally written by Michael Wilson had turned out poorly, and a new British playwright with no previous screenplay writing experience was hired. His name was Robert Bolt, and his historical drama *A Man for All Seasons* was the best play currently in the West End. Bolt's poetic dialogue and his fine-tuned sense of historical drama gave the *Lawrence* script a beauty and intelligence never before heard in an epic. For once a sweeping saga would be as magnificent to hear as it was to see. As Bolt worked away, and Lean set off scouting locations in Jordan and Egypt, Spiegel continued to search for his Lawrence.

Once more Sam Spiegel announced a new star for his desert epic. Lawrence would be played by newcomer Albert Finney. Finney had been part of the Royal Court Theatre group and had appeared in *The Entertainer* with Laurence Olivier. But in 1960 he was virtually unknown by the general public. Lean was pleased with Finney's rather extensive screen tests. But after four days of working, Finney quit the production, telling Lean he wasn't interested in becoming an international film star, nor in working in the desert for a year. Lean thought Finney's decision was also brought on by Spiegel's insistence that the young actor sign an exclusive five-year contract with the producer. Nonetheless, Finney was gone. Oddly enough, two years later Finney made an "art house" film in which he took a third of the ownership, along with its director, Tony Richardson, and its writer, John Osborne. The film was *Tom Jones,* which made all three millionaires and turned Finney into just what he had professed he hadn't wanted to become—an international film star. The search for Lawrence continued.

Lean returned to Brando, who once again refused. He considered Laurence Harvey, Anthony Perkins, and Richard Burton, but for various reasons none of them seemed ideal. Montgomery Clift began campaigning for the part, telephoning Lean weekly, begging for the role. As the start date grew closer, the rest of the cast was filling in nicely, including Alec Guinness as Prince Feisal, Anthony Quinn as Abu, Claude Rains as Dryden, Anthony Quayle as Colonel Brighton, and Edmond O'Brien as Bentley, a journalist based on Lowell Thomas. (An ailing O'Brien was eventually replaced by Arthur Kennedy.) The pivotal role of Sheik Ali went to a young Egyptian star named Omar Sharif, although Christian Marquand had been in the running.

After an exhaustive search, Lean finally took a tip from his great friend Katharine Hepburn on a young actor she'd seen at the Royal Court in *The Long and the Short and the Tall.* The actor was Peter O'Toole. Lean, who had directed Hepburn stunningly in *Summertime* several years before, trusted her instincts and called in O'Toole for a test. Anne V. Coates, Lean's editor on *Lawrence,* remembers the screen test vividly. O'Toole had bleached his hair blond, the color it would be in the film, and although he was much taller than the real Lawrence, it made no difference. In front of the cameras O'Toole *was* Lawrence, every facet of his complex and varied personality superbly realized. He was Lawrence the warrior, the child on an adventure, the sadistic soldier, and the lonely homosexual who mistakenly thought he had become a god in the Arabian deserts. His eyes had an astonishing poetry to them that perfectly suited Bolt's special dialogue. By the end of the screen test, Lean and Spiegel knew they had found their Lawrence, and Peter O'Toole was signed to star.

Shooting began in May 1961 and would end in October of the following year. Upon Katharine Hepburn's urging, O'Toole had his nose fixed before filming, which softened his features and made him look even more like Lawrence in spirit. The filming of *Lawrence of Arabia* was as epic as the story they were telling, but everyone sensed the importance of what was being created. Lean's direction was his best yet. Freddie Young's camera work was beyond anything most people could imagine. If nothing else, Lean and Young would capture the desert in a way no one had ever quite seen before. The cost was over $14 million, large for 1962 but not outrageously so. (By today's standards it would probably cost close to $150 million to duplicate the exact same production.) Lean quickly edited and scored the film in October and November, and it had its world premiere before Queen Elizabeth II and Prince Philip in London on December 9, 1962. It was initially met with mixed critical reaction, many scoffing at its four-hours-plus running time. But no one could fault the powerhouse performance by Peter O'Toole. He *was* Lawrence and, after the film's release, a major star.

Lawrence of Arabia opened two weeks later in New York, Los Angeles, Washington, D.C., and Toronto, to mixed reviews, but the word of mouth was sensational. Within days it was selling out, and by the end of the Christmas season it was obvious that *Lawrence* was the film of the year and Peter O'Toole the brightest new discovery. David Lean had done it again.

Lawrence of Arabia was nominated for ten Academy Awards, including one for Peter O'Toole as Best Actor and another for Omar Sharif as Best Supporting Actor. Both Lean and the film won awards, along with five others for cinematography, music, art direction, editing, and costume design; but Peter O'Toole lost to a previous four-time loser, Gregory Peck, for his work in the popular screen version of Harper Lee's best-selling novel *To Kill a Mockingbird*. Looking back, it's hard to believe O'Toole lost. He was to be nominated six more times, making him a seven-time loser, along with Richard Burton.

O'Toole went on to play Henry II in *Becket*, a part he'd had to give up on stage in order to play Lawrence. He once again played Henry II in *The Lion in Winter*. His Mr. Chips was memorable, and his zany antics in *The Ruling Class* just one more jewel in an illustrious career. Eventually his private life caught up with him, and now he is no longer able to drink. He looks exceedingly haggard for his years, as recently witnessed in his stage appearance in London in a play by Keith Waterhouse. But even now there's a flash in his eyes and a fire in his voice, and suddenly you can see behind all the abuse the robust and mercurial young star who made *Lawrence of Arabia* one of the greatest films of all time.

There has always existed a love-hate relationship between Broadway and Hollywood. Though the stage has provided a continual source of material for the movies, especially after the advent of sound, what was superb in the theater has often ended up turgid on film.

There are many reasons for this. Some plays just aren't particularly adaptable, such as the works of Eugene O'Neill—with the possible exception of *Long Day's Journey into Night* (1962), which, for all its brilliance, remained a photographed play. On the other hand, Lillian Hellman's and Tennessee Williams's works have had a high rate of success when transferred to the screen. William Wyler's version of Hellman's *The Little Foxes,* which the playwright adapted to the screen, was every bit as fine as the 1939 stage production. Elia Kazan's production of *A Streetcar Named Desire* (1951) was every bit as scorching and sensational as the 1947 stage version. In both cases a number of important elements were retained from the Broadway productions. *Streetcar* had the same writer and director and three of the four original cast members.

One example of a screen musical that captured the vitality of the Broadway original is *The King and I*. Yul Brynner starred in both versions, and his memorable performance as the king of Siam elevated the material immeasurably. Another example is the 1972 film version of Hal Prince's 1966 musical hit *Cabaret;* director Bob Fosse's innovative approach in reworking the original Christopher Isherwood stories into the material wisely gave the movie an edge and bite missing from the stage production. Unfortunately there have been more disastrous transitions than successful ones; *The Glass Menagerie, Man of La Mancha,* and *A Chorus Line* are just three of many such duds.

One legitimate reason for this problem may lie in the Holly-

Audrey Hepburn was castigated for not singing in My Fair Lady, *but no one could deny her appealing charm and elegance.*

wood tradition of replacing perhaps lesser-known Broadway actors with better-known but not better-suited Hollywood stars. Ethel Merman reached the pinnacle of her magnificent career in the 1959 musical *Gypsy,* playing the tyrannical stage mother of the fabulous queen of the striptease, Gypsy Rose Lee. But when Mervyn LeRoy filmed the musical in 1962, he passed over Miss Merman for the nonsinging Rosalind Russell. Both the film and Miss Russell were sad in comparison. The peerless Mary Martin became a Broadway legend with her portrayal of Nellie Forbush in the Pulitzer Prize–winning Rodgers and Hammerstein musical *South Pacific.* But producer Buddy Adler felt Miss Martin was too old to play the part convincingly on screen when he produced the 1958 film. Mitzi Gaynor was cast instead and proved merely adequate, no more and no less. The film was successful at the box office with its presold title, but it sorely lacked the magic of the original play. Carol Channing had her finest moment playing the middle-aged matchmaking busybody in Gower Champion's sparkling 1964 musical smash *Hello, Dolly,* yet when Gene Kelly directed the bloated 1969 screen version, Miss Channing was replaced by a much younger Barbra Streisand, fresh from her Oscar-winning triumph in *Funny Girl.* Miss Streisand was clearly a more potent box office draw but was unmistakably miscast, and as hard as she tried, the film failed miserably.

Still, no greater outcry was heard than when Jack Warner announced Audrey Hepburn as Eliza Doolittle in the 1964 film version of Lerner and Loewe's stunning musical of George Bernard Shaw's great play *Pygmalion,* now called *My Fair Lady.* Journalists all over the country couldn't believe Warner had passed over the original Eliza, the delightful Julie Andrews, who had yet to make a screen appearance.

My Fair Lady began with Shaw's film version of *Pygmalion.* That pantheon playwright of the British theater had initially nixed the many offers to film his extensive list of plays. He distrusted the medium. Strangely enough, Shaw couldn't resist the considerable charms of a little-known Hungarian impresario, Gabriel Pascal, granting him permission to produce film versions of no less than four of Shaw's plays, beginning with the 1938 production of *Pygmalion*. Shaw was commissioned to script the adaptation, although he had never read a screenplay in his life. He asked one question: How long did a film comedy generally run? He was told around ninety minutes. Thus, with a brilliantly prudent pen, Shaw cut his three-hour stage opus into a film with a running time of a little over ninety minutes. Leslie Howard played Henry Higgins to perfection, and a young Wendy Hiller was introduced to the world as the cockney flower girl Eliza Doolittle. Hiller was personally selected by Shaw for the role. Anthony Asquith directed and David Lean edited, and the results were delicious. Over the following fifteen years, several producers attempted to buy the rights for a musical version, including Rodgers and Hammerstein. Finally Herman Levin secured the rights from Pascal and interested the team of Alan Jay Lerner and Frederick Loewe to write the book and music for the stage version, now called *My Fair Lady*. Lerner and Loewe had won acclaim for two musicals, *Brigadoon* and *Paint Your Wagon*. Lerner also had won an Oscar for his original screenplay for the award-winning *An American in Paris*. Lerner cleverly latched on to the screenplay by Shaw, which was a perfect ninety-minute length, and used this as his book to the musical. Thus, with the songs, the evening would run a normal two and a half hours. In an inspired piece of casting, Rex Harrison played Henry Higgins, and he was forever associated with the part, giving one of the ultimate Shavian performances of the century. And for the coveted role of Eliza Doolittle, a very young British musical comedy star, currently on Broadway in *The Boy Friend,* was selected. Her name was Julie Andrews. With a strong hand Moss Hart directed Miss Andrews, and the production, into musical comedy history. Miss Andrews not only sang the part superbly, but was every bit as good in the dramatic end, matching Rex Harrison quite competently. No other musical perhaps has had a score that so perfectly suited the book. No other musical had a book quite as rich as this one. And nothing ever looked quite as glorious on stage as Cecil Beaton's designs. *My Fair Lady* ran for seven and a half years in New York and five years in London. It played all over the world. The album was a best-seller for two years running in the number one position. The play won the Tony Award, the Grammy Award for Best Album, and the New York Critics Award as Best Musical of 1956.

Jack L. Warner, the rapacious autocrat of Warner Brothers Studio, happened to be in the audience opening night of *My Fair Lady* and from that moment on pursued Levin and CBS, who had put up all the money for the stage play in order to have the album rights, into selling the project to him for the film version. He eventually wore them down and, with an offer of $5.5 million, obtained the rights to the play, the highest amount ever paid for a musical at the time. After initially flirting with Vin-

Hepburn as the flower girl to Rex Harrison's Oscar-winning professor of speech, Henry Higgins.

cente Minnelli and Jerome Robbins, Warner selected George Cukor to direct the screen version. It was a choice assignment. Alan Jay Lerner was retained to write the script and Cecil Beaton to design the sets and costumes.

Now came time for the casting, which fell to Jack Warner as the film's producer. It was naturally assumed Rex Harrison would repeat his role as Higgins, but this was not the case. Cukor's and Lerner's first choice was a then unknown Peter O'Toole. They had heard of his incredible performance as the tortured T. E. Lawrence in the yet-to-be-released epic *Lawrence of Arabia,* and after seeing rushes of his performance, they convinced Warner to make O'Toole an offer. O'Toole accepted immediately, but when his agent asked for a big salary and a percentage of the box office, Warner squashed the deal, and Peter O'Toole was no longer in the running. (O'Toole was to successfully play Henry Higgins in a 1978 London and New York stage production.) Warner next brainstormed the notion of Cary Grant playing Higgins. Cukor was aghast by this idea. After all, Grant was a Cockney himself, hardly the sort to be playing the aristocratic Higgins. (Cukor had dealt before with Cary Grant playing Norman Maine to Judy Garland's Vicki Lester in his superb 1954 musical version of *A Star Is Born,* but Grant had backed out, feeling the role was too unsympathetic. Cukor never quite forgave Grant for this.) Warner also thought of James Cagney to play Alfred Doolittle, Eliza's shiftless father, a role Stanley Holloway had established to great acclaim in both New York and London. (Cagney, who had recently retired from films, stayed wisely in retirement, and Holloway repeated his Doolittle in the film, winning an Oscar nomination for Best Supporting Actor.) Cary Grant responded to Warner's offer by saying if Rex Harrison didn't play the part of Henry Higgins, he wouldn't even go see the film of *My Fair Lady.* Warner listened, and much to Cukor's and Lerner's relief, Harrison was cast as Henry Higgins.

Alan Jay Lerner was especially keen on seeing Julie Andrews re-create her role in the film version. In his mind, she was his creation, his Eliza. He had selected her to play the role and made a great Broadway star out of her. She had played the queen in his next Broadway musical, *Camelot,* and had won rave reviews, showing new depths as an actress. What's more, she could really sing the part. But she had never made a film before, and outside of the theatergoing audiences of New York and London, she was an unknown commodity. Jack Warner bitterly fought Lerner and Cukor on the Julie Andrews issue, saying he'd paid too much money for the project not to have some kind of box office insurance. He had said yes to Rex Harrison, who meant nothing at the box office. Warner simply would not have two stars of no box office value in an eventual $17 million production. He proposed one of the biggest stars in Hollywood, Audrey Hepburn, although her only previous musical experience, *Funny Face* with Fred Astaire, had shown she could hardly keep a tune. But Hepburn, ever since dazzling audiences with her Academy Award–winning debut in *Roman Holiday,* was the biggest star in Hollywood outside of Elizabeth Taylor and Marilyn Monroe. She had been nominated four times for an Academy Award, most recently as Holly Golightly in *Breakfast at Tiffany's,* and Jack Warner was determined to have her. With an offer of $1 million to play Eliza Doolittle, Hepburn accepted the role. She telephoned Julie Andrews and simply admitted she couldn't resist the offer. Andrews, although bitterly disappointed, understood Hepburn's position and even recognized Warner's logic in not using her. After Hepburn was cast, Alan Jay Lerner lost complete interest in the film and hardly had anything to do with it.

The press was outraged at the slight. Sheila Graham thought Jack Warner had lost his mind. Every Broadway columnist indignantly criticized Hepburn's replacement of Andrews, particularly when it was announced that Marni Nixon would dub all the singing for Hepburn in the film. Nevertheless, filming began on *My Fair Lady* in 1963, with Rex Harrison and Audrey Hepburn.

As for Julie Andrews, well, during the run of *Camelot* the one and only Walt Disney came backstage after one performance and offered her the plum part of the fantastic English nanny Mary Poppins. Miss Andrews said she was interested but didn't pay much attention after not hearing from Disney for quite a while. Thus, after she lost the part of Eliza, Disney was once again there, ready to commence production with his most lavish film yet, *Mary Poppins*. This time a firm offer was made, so while Audrey Hepburn was re-creating Eliza Doolittle on the sound stages of Warner Brothers in Burbank, California, Julie Andrews was making her screen debut filming *Mary Poppins* at Disney just a mile away.

The release of *My Fair Lady* in 1964 was the biggest film event of the year. But part of its thunder was stolen when *Mary Poppins* opened in June of the same year. The critics were ecstatic about Julie Andrews and the film. It quickly became Disney's greatest hit to date, and everywhere you went everyone was talking about Julie Andrews. After *Poppins* Andrews won the part of Maria von Trapp in the enormous production of *The Sound of Music,* which she filmed in 1964. In retrospect, perhaps everyone was a little overly generous to Miss Andrews in *Mary Poppins* out of consideration for her loss in not playing Eliza Doolittle. *Poppins* is fine, and Miss Andrews is fine, but it's hardly a shattering performance. It's sweet and charming, but not a revelation. Andrews was to prove her talents beyond all expectations in her next film, *The Sound of Music.* So in October of 1964, *My Fair Lady* opened to rave reviews for all concerned. It had duplicated the stage play to a tee, perhaps being too faithful in some people's mind. Rex Harrison was praised to the hills, and Audrey Hepburn proved to be a radiant Eliza. But she was sorely criticized by many for not doing her own singing. Some even felt it hurt her performance and the film. Still, when it came right down to it, Audrey Hepburn was breathtaking.

At Oscar time *My Fair Lady* was bestowed with twelve nominations. Everyone was honored, including Rex Harrison for Best Actor. The only major exclusion was Audrey Hepburn. She was not nominated for her performance as Eliza. The only other film to beat out *My Fair Lady* for nominations was *Mary Poppins* with thirteen, including one for Julie Andrews for Best Actress. Nonetheless, Miss Hepburn graciously agreed to attend the gala event and hand out the Best Actor award.

On the night of the awards ceremony, Julie Andrews won Best Actress for *Mary Poppins*. In her acceptance speech, she thanked Jack Warner for making it all happen. She acknowledged what everyone already knew. She had won the award for not being in *My Fair Lady*. Meanwhile *My Fair Lady* won eight Oscars, including Best Picture and Best Director, and Audrey Hepburn presented Rex Harrison with the award for Best Actor.

My Fair Lady was to be one of Audrey Hepburn's last major roles. Three years later she retired from the screen. Although she attempted to revive her career nearly ten years later, she never again attracted the parts she had had in the past. Still, she was one of the best-loved actresses of all time. She died of cancer in 1993.

Rex Harrison had a long, successful film and stage career, even reviving *My Fair Lady* in 1980 on Broadway and around the United States. He was active until his death in 1989.

Julie Andrews is still in films, but her career never took off the way it did in the mid-1960s. She was forever saddled with the sugary image of Mary Poppins, and audiences couldn't quite accept her as anything else. But to this day she is grateful to Jack Warner for not casting her in *My Fair Lady*. Without knowing it, he gave her a wonderful start to her film career, with an Oscar to boot.

The founding fathers of the Hollywood studio system felt that each of their own particular fiefdoms was very much a family affair. Thus, during this period—the twenties and thirties—nepotism reached a kind of glossy pinnacle in tinsel town. The hungry, ambitious, and sometimes even semitalented young men making their way up through the Hollywood ranks found it enormously advantageous if their wives were a movie czar's daughter or perhaps an actual movie star herself.

Take Douglas Shearer, for starters. With the realization that talkies were here to stay, Louis B. Mayer created the sound department at Metro-Goldwyn-Mayer. He hired Douglas Shearer to head the department, a task Shearer performed quite brilliantly at times over the next forty years. Of course, Mr. Shearer's appointment was facilitated by the fact that his sister, Norma, was the acknowledged queen of the M-G-M lot and his brother-in-law, Irving Thalberg, was the studio's boy-genius head of production. When Darryl F. Zanuck ran 20th Century–Fox, he hired his own son, Richard, to head up production during the 1960s (a move that would later turn into a showdown where Zanuck the elder would fire Zanuck the younger as production head). Finally, when Louis B. Mayer selected his eldest daughter's young husband, David O. Selznick, to help run M-G-M for the then ailing Irving Thalberg, detractors cried out sharply, "The son-in-law also rises!"

In the 1960s, however, when the American New Wave commenced with the 1967 release of Arthur Penn and Warren Beatty's revisionist gangster classic *Bonnie and Clyde,* Hollywood nepotism was on the wane. It was the dawn of the film school graduate as major Hollywood player. Suddenly it was better to have a diploma from the UCLA Film School than a niece of Harry Cohn as your wife. And although nepotism never disappeared from Hollywood—in fact, it's still running strong—the film school graduate has given nepotism a run for its money. Film school studies were a late postwar phenomenon, available primarily on campuses in New York and Los Angeles. Its students were second-generation film lovers, men and women whose lives had been profoundly influenced and shaped by the images they viewed. And whereas the French New Wave of the late 1950s pulled many of its finest innovators—Truffaut, Godard, and Chabrol—from the realm of film criticism (all three were formerly critics for the famed *Cahiers du Cinéma*), the American New Wave of the 1960s recruited an overwhelming number of its participants fresh from the budding film schools at several of the nation's finest colleges. One in particular seems to have been especially blessed: the USC Film School spawned the future creator of the *Star Wars* and *Raiders of the Lost Ark* series, George Lucas; our generation's Cecil B. De Mille, Steven Spielberg *(E.T., Jaws);* and Spielberg's protégé, Robert Zemeckis, who eventually would surpass his mentor's inventiveness with his 1988 breakthrough film, *Who Framed Roger Rabbit.* Interestingly enough, these three producer/directors have been responsible for nearly half of the top-twenty-grossing films of all time.

Others on the film school graduate honor roll would have to include film directors Martin Scorsese *(Raging Bull),* Brian De Palma *(Carrie),* John Milius *(The Wind and the Lion),* and Terrence Malick *(Days of Heaven)*—all of them achieving importance during the seventies.

But the film school graduate par excellence is, without a doubt, Francis Ford Coppola, a cinematic dynamo whose name above the title eventually became synonymous with the best Hollywood studio films could deliver. The four films Coppola produced, directed, and wrote during the seventies represent the apex of American filmmaking. *The Godfather* quickly became one of the most successful films of all time, entering into the nation's cultural fabric and winning the Academy Award for Best Picture of 1972, along with an award for Coppola and

The genius behind Apocalypse Now, *Francis Ford Coppola.*

Mario Puzo's screenplay and another for Marlon Brando as Best Actor for his amazing comeback performance as Don Corleone, the Godfather. Coppola followed this with a small film about wiretappers, a political nightmare that ranks with Kafka's *The Trial,* called *The Conversation,* starring Gene Hackman. This film was nominated for Best Picture of 1974 by the Academy of Motion Picture Arts and Sciences, along with another nomination for Coppola's original screenplay. *The Conversation* lost all of its nominations to the main contender of the evening, *The Godfather, Part II,* produced, directed, and cowritten by Francis Ford Coppola. Coppola's sequel proved to be the exception to the rule—vastly superior to the already sensational original. *The Godfather, Part II* was a deep, multilayered treatise on the corruption of the soul and how the sins of the father return to corrupt the seeds in his sons. It was unsparing, poetic, and expertly edited.

The acting in *The Godfather, Part II* was exceptional, particularly that of Robert De Niro as the young Don Corleone. Pauline Kael, grande dame of film criticism, immediately championed Coppola's achievement, placing him at the forefront of American directors. *The Godfather, Part II* was honored with Academy Awards to its writer and director (Francis Coppola); its supporting actor Robert De Niro; its musical score, cowritten by Coppola's father, Carmine, along with Nino Rota; its costume designs; and, finally, its production. With the award of Best Picture for 1974, Coppola received his third victory of the evening as Best Producer. It was the first and only time thus far that both a film and its sequel won Oscars as Best Picture of the year.

As 1975 began, Francis Ford Coppola was the most highly regarded American filmmaker in the world. He rejuvenated his own production company, American Zoetrope, in San Francisco, where he planned to make films outside the Hollywood system. Coppola has reserved playing the role of producer for

Jack Nicholson was offered the role of either Willard or Kurtz, but he turned them both down.

films made by fellow film school graduate George Lucas and other close associates. The first such venture was a science fiction film called *THX-1138,* which failed at the box office. With his new-gained clout after *The Godfather* success, Coppola next produced, for Universal Studios, George Lucas's newest effort, a nostalgic comedy about the last night of summer vacation in Modesto, California, in 1962. Upon its completion, Ned Tanen, then head of production for Universal, viewed the film and hated what he saw. Tanen immediately thought of shelving the film. Coppola violently disagreed with Tanen's assessment. Championing the film, Coppola exerted enormous pressure on Universal until Tanen caved in and, in the summer of 1973, released *American Graffiti,* although he was positive it would last less than two weeks. He was wrong. Audiences embraced *American Graffiti,* making it the studio's biggest money maker of that year. It received no less than five Academy Award nominations, including one for Best Picture and another for Best Director. Five years later an unsuccessful sequel, *More American Graffiti,* was released. Today *American Graffiti* remains a classic American comedy. Everyone agreed Coppola had the golden touch. Now just what was he planning on doing with it?

Coppola announced his intention to make a Vietnam movie based on a script purchased by American Zoetrope in 1969. It was entitled *Apocalypse Now* and had been written by John Milius. Based loosely on Joseph Conrad's gripping novella *Heart of Darkness,* the film would commence shooting in the spring of 1976, with United Artists financing its original $13 million budget.

Joseph Conrad is one of the recognized masters of modern literature, and *Heart of Darkness,* a treatise on the very nature of evil hiding in every human heart, is often considered his masterwork. In this unusually thrilling and often frightening adventure, Conrad thrusts the reader, through an astounding literary journey, into the very depths of the soul. His protagonist, sea captain Marlowe, snakes up the Congo River, running through the darkest unknown regions of equatorial Africa in search of the mysterious Kurtz, a European ivory trader who is thought to have "gone native" and is very possibly insane. Ultimately Marlowe confronts Kurtz and the inherent demons alive and well within every human heart. And although Kurtz has succumbed to "the horror" of his life, Marlowe finds salvation in recognizing the evil just below the surface of his own skin. Compact in length, but epic in scope and spiritual implications, *Heart of Darkness* is also one hell of an adventure yarn.

In 1939 a young Orson Welles came to Hollywood to make motion pictures for RKO, announcing for his initial feature *Heart of Darkness,* based on his successful radio production performed by the Mercury Players. It was Welles's intention to play both Marlowe and Kurtz, but in the end he abandoned *Heart of Darkness* in favor of another film—this one about a newspaper tycoon, first entitled *An American* and later called *Citizen Kane.*

For the next thirty years several attempts were made to film *Heart of Darkness,* but nothing materialized. Then, in 1969, during the height of the Vietnam War, John Milius, one of the stars of the film school graduates, wrote a script, a variation of *Heart of Darkness* now set in Vietnam and wonderfully titled *Apocalypse Now.* Coppola's recently created production company, American Zoetrope, optioned the screenplay, with George Lucas set to direct.

Milius's script follows Conrad's basic structure and plot. Marlowe is now Willard, a captain used by the Special Military Services as an in-house assassin. Kurtz is a Green Beret colonel, illegally operating in Cambodia with his own renegade army. According to U.S. military intelligence, Kurtz is clearly insane. Willard is to find the colonel and "terminate him with extreme prejudice." Along his journey to Kurtz, Willard meets Captain Kilgore, a "madman" who loves war and surfing and is probably the finest officer the army can produce. (The part was memorably played by Robert Duvall in the film.)

That is about all of Milius's original script that remains in *Apocalypse Now*. For all intents and purposes, Coppola is the author of *Apocalypse Now,* although he generously shared a cowriting credit with Milius. (Strangely enough, Milius petitioned the Writers Guild, saying his screenplay of *Apocalypse Now* was an original and not based on *Heart of Darkness.* The Writers Guild ruled in favor of Mr. Milius's request!) By 1975 Coppola was set to direct and produce *Apocalypse Now.* Its original director, George Lucas, went on to make his science fiction fantasy *Star Wars* and lived comfortably ever after off the profits.

Casting for *Apocalypse Now* began in the fall of 1975. Initially Coppola wanted Steve McQueen to play Captain Willard. But McQueen didn't like the idea of spending so much time filming on location, away from his new bride, actress Ali MacGraw. After he passed, Jack Nicholson was approached, but he too

Dennis Hopper, Martin Sheen, and Frederic Forrest in Apocalypse Now.

turned down Coppola. So Francis hired a relatively little-known actor of terrific promise, Harvey Keitel. Keitel had recently made a critical impact with his performance in Martin Scorsese's autobiographical film *Mean Streets* (1973). He was used again effectively as a chilling womanizer in Scorsese's wonderful comedy *Alice Doesn't Live Here Anymore* (1974). Physically Keitel was well suited for the role of Willard: compact, lean, and with almost visible killer instincts. Still, more important, after a difficult negotiation, Marlon Brando joined the company in the role of Colonel Kurtz. The star and director of *The Godfather* were reunited. Brando also agreed to play the part for a mere three weeks at a record-breaking fee of $3 million. In good faith, Brando asked for and received a million dollars in advance. The rest of the cast included Larry Fishburne, Sam Bottoms, Albert Hall, Frederic Forrest, and, in a small part, a young Harrison Ford. Ford was used by Coppola previously in *The Conversation* and *American Graffiti*. Ford filmed his part in *Apocalypse Now* before playing Han Solo in *Star Wars*. Because of delays on *Apocalypse Now,* by the time the film reached the screen in 1979 Harrison Ford was well on his way to becoming a major movie star.

Thus, after months and months of preproduction, *Apocalypse Now* began shooting in April of 1976 in the Philippines without benefit of a completed script. Even worse, the actual filming was so heavily plagued with disasters that its completion required a Herculean effort. It was as if nature had declared war on Coppola's production cast and crew. Hurricanes, typhoons, floods, walls of humidity, and armies of bugs became an accepted part of life.

The first major shake-up occurred just after the first full week of shooting. Coppola reviewed all the printed footage for the week and, based on what he saw, decided to fire Harvey Keitel, which meant finding an immediate replacement. No one has ever really said what went wrong with Keitel, but his interpretation of Willard was obviously not Coppola's. Keitel was quickly paid off, and a small column on his dismissal made the front page of the *Daily Variety*. Meanwhile Coppola wasted no time in flying to Los Angeles, where he conducted a meeting at the airport with actor Martin Sheen. Sheen was one of the best young actors in the business. He had gained national attention with his performance as the Irish son returning home from World War II in Frank D. Gilroy's Pulitzer Prize–winning drama *The Subject Was Roses,* creating the role both on Broadway and in the Oscar-winning screen version. As the psychotic young James Dean wannabe killer, Sheen impressed the critics in the cult classic *Badlands.* But he won the most public recognition for his television appearances, especially as Robert Kennedy in the award-winning miniseries "The Missiles of October."

Casting Martin Sheen as Captain Willard made sense. His baby face with its wide-eyed innocent stare and his all-American good looks made Sheen an immediately likable figure. But as Sheen proved so expertly in *Badlands,* there's actually a steely cold killer underneath that childlike exterior. This volatile and unexpected combination was just the spark needed to ignite the character of Captain Willard.

When the meeting of the two men drew to a close, Coppola had managed to seduce Sheen into playing Willard. In retrospect, Sheen understands his reasons for saying yes to Coppola and the sheer folly of undertaking such an assignment. The thirty-nine-year-old actor was in the worst physical condition of his life. He was smoking three packs of cigarettes a day. And here he was, playing the toughest role of his entire screen career. He felt he could quickly get back in shape and probably handle the rigorous sixteen-week shooting schedule Coppola had promised. Little did he suspect how far off Coppola's projection was—shooting would run over schedule by a year—and just how dearly that overtime would cost Sheen.

Filming once again resumed in the Philippines. Coppola was especially pleased by Sheen's bold, on-the-edge performance. The agonizing, soul-bared hotel scene early in the film was so intense, the drunken actor didn't realize he had actually slit his wrists on the jagged bits of broken mirror. With his soul in the very vortex of hell, Sheen collapsed in tears, wrapped in a bloodstained bedsheet, creating a moment so real and personal that it's hard to watch. But it is Martin Sheen's finest moment on film.

Growing immeasurably in its magnitude, the cast and crew battled on under General Coppola's sword swift guidance. But the production was delayed because of a month-long downpour of torrential rains, followed by an encounter with a nasty typhoon that destroyed many of the sets. The actors and crew became frayed by the heat, the delays, the long hours, and a constant flow of drugs on the set. Indeed, the surrealism of the war they were depicting infiltrated the entire company. Everyone seemed inspired by a fine madness—no one more so than Martin Sheen, who *became* Willard, the agonized sinner sliding up and down the razor's edge of life. Sheen became so consumed that people around him started to worry about his mental health. And throughout all of this, Coppola continued furiously to rewrite the script, incorporating far more of Conrad's *Heart of Darkness* into the film's themes and narrative structure. Still, the producer was unable to write a satisfying ending.

These complications left the film months behind schedule and $3 million overbudget, with no end in sight. When it became apparent that Coppola would be unable to honor the negotiated shooting dates with Brando, he asked for an extension to accommodate the film's fluctuating schedule. Brando refused and threatened to quit the film, although he was unwilling to return his million-dollar advance. Stung by such inflexibility, Coppola refused to be bullied by Brando's selfish tactics and struck back by suggesting they recast Colonel Kurtz with one of the original choices for the part: Robert Redford, Jack Nicholson, or Al Pacino. When Brando's agent heard about this, he urged his client to reconsider. Brando made amends and agreed to shoot his three-week stretch later on.

Apocalypse Now had been before the cameras for nearly a year when on March 1, 1977, Martin Sheen was rushed to the hospital with severe chest pains. He had had a massive heart attack, undoubtedly brought on by three packs of cigarettes a day, by the strain and stress of the production, and, in a curious way, by Captain Willard himself. The severity of the attack was, initially, so grave that Sheen received his last rites from a local priest.

Coppola thus found himself facing one of the worst crises a director could ever know while in the midst of shooting a film—the sudden death of a leading actor or actress. One solution was to recast the part and reshoot the previously completed scenes, but this was out of the question on a production with a budget now twice its original figure and nearly nine months behind schedule. So Coppola kept the whole thing as quiet as possible and started shooting around Martin Sheen, who was now in a hospital in Los Angeles. After three weeks there was nothing left to shoot, so they began using doubles for Sheen, photographing him only from the rear. Meanwhile the press began leaking stories about Coppola's Vietnam folly, especially after United Artists canceled its original release date in late 1977. Finally, six weeks after his attack, Sheen returned to the set and filming resumed. It's to the credit of both actor and director that Sheen's real-life ordeal didn't alter the intensity of his performance. In fact, it added a kind of otherworldliness to Sheen's face.

Martin Sheen's return in no way circumvented Coppola's merciless parade of production problems. He was never able to overcome his difficulties with finding a way to end the film, so even when a three-hundred-pound Marlon Brando arrived with his entourage of Polynesian women, there was still no conclusion. For the next three weeks, under Coppola's encouragement, Brando and Sheen improvised various scenes and possible endings. Coppola also realized he was now photographing a man who was about the same size as Rhode Island, so he thought it best to keep Brando seated throughout most of the improvised scenes. A double was used for Brandon's long shots to save the actor from any public embarrassment. Just how successful these three-week improvisations were is hard to tell since only about ten minutes of them appear in the final film.

Finally, after fifteen months of location shooting, principal photography on *Apocalypse Now* concluded in June of 1977 at a cost of nearly three times its original budget and a year overschedule. United Artists was worried about their investment, but no more so than Francis Ford Coppola, who had stuck every dollar he had into the film's escalating costs.

By the time *Apocalypse Now* reached the screen in the summer of 1979, it had already missed two scheduled opening dates and had lost some of its thunder when another Vietnam story, *The Deer Hunter,* had swept the Academy Awards, winning Best Director and Best Picture of 1978. *Apocalypse Now* became the "second" Vietnam movie. Even as late as early May, Coppola wasn't happy with the film's ending, so he held two showings in Westwood, California, asking the paying public audiences to fill out extensive questionnaires detailing their reaction to the film. (Although in 1979 this was quite a maverick gesture, it has since become an accepted strategy in test-marketing films.)

Apocalypse Now was screened for two sold-out performances with the more pessimistic ending. This was an ending that might stir up a debate among intellectuals, but it left the average moviegoing viewer baffled and unhappy. But the overwhelming response was one of amazement. The audiences had clearly been electrified. Based on this response, Coppola presented *Apocalypse Now* at the Cannes Film Festival, placing it in competition but calling it a "work in progress." It won the Grand Prize, the Palm d'Oro, for Best Picture, sharing this distinction with the German film version of Gunter Grass's *The Tin Drum*. Francis Ford Coppola returned from Europe triumphant. What was once considered his folly was now turning into his masterpiece.

Apocalypse Now was met with mixed feelings critically. Some preferred the macho myth of *The Deer Hunter*. Others felt the ending was a cheat, and Brando's Kurtz ultimately didn't add up to much. Still another group of critics was dazzled by the sheer audacity and power of the film, particularly a spectacular battle scene underscored by the music of Wagner. Everyone loved Robert Duvall, and the physical production was of course greatly admired. But the critics seemed hesitant to totally embrace the film.

If Hollywood insiders were playing coy in their reaction to Coppola's four-year undertaking, the public was going just plain nuts. This film struck a chord, especially with the baby boom generation. Thus, from the day of its release, *Apocalypse Now* was a hit, quickly making back all that it had cost and returning quite a handsome investment to United Artists as well as to Francis Ford Coppola.

The film was eventually nominated for nine Academy Awards, including Best Picture and Best Director. And for all the pain and suffering Martin Sheen had endured, he was none-theless passed over by the academy for a Best Actor nomination. The film took home only two awards—one for cinematography and another for sound—losing all the major categories to that first true yuppie melodrama, *Kramer vs. Kramer,* which was a fine film but hardly in the same league as Coppola's epic.

Today, all those involved in this film consider it one of the greatest experiences they ever had. *Apocalypse Now* is recognized as a milestone in American filmmaking and is perhaps the last great movie Coppola ever directed. He has yet to equal it. Martin Sheen never achieved the kind of stardom one might have expected after *Apocalypse Now*, but he remains an active performer in both films and television. But even he admits that this particular film was a kind of apex in his career. It's unlikely he'll ever do another one quite like it again.

On October 13, 1962, a theatrical explosion rocked the Billy Rose Theatre, and Broadway has been picking up the loose pieces ever since. It was a lacerating four-character, one-set, three-act drama by off-Broadway's avant-garde wunderkind Edward Albee, and it was brilliantly entitled *Who's Afraid of Virginia Woolf?*—a coy satire on the song "Who's Afraid of the Big Bad Wolf?" and an enigmatic literary reference to the inevitable but no less painful blows of day-to-day reality. Audiences were horrified, stunned, but finally transfixed by this three-and-a-half-hour marathon of verbal assaults between an older college campus couple—George, an associate professor of history, and his shrewish older wife, Martha, who happens to be the college dean's daughter—and a younger, newly arrived college campus couple—Nick, a good-looking biology professor, and his frumpy wife, Honey. The play starts late one Saturday night and ends at dawn, playing in "real time," as it were. The dialogue and situations spewed forth in *Who's Afraid of Virginia Woolf?* contained more obscenities and vulgarities than all the other

American plays of the previous decade combined. Throughout the night the couples indulge in such games as "Get the Guests," "Humiliate the Host," "Hump the Hostess," and, finally, "Bringing Up Baby," which by its conclusion has forever shattered the lives of these four characters, changing them irrevocably. The same went for much of the audience who witnessed the original production with landmark performances in the American Theatre from Uta Hagen and Arthur Hill as Martha and George.

Hollywood's premiere acting couple Elizabeth Taylor and Richard Burton reached the pinnacles of their careers in Who's Afraid of Virginia Woolf, *though both were thought to be miscast.*

Who's Afraid of Virginia Woolf? quickly became the most successful and discussed drama of the year, with everyone speculating on its exact meaning and dozens of explanations offered by theater critics and commentators everywhere. Suddenly Edward Albee became *the* most celebrated playwright in America, heir apparent not only to Tennessee Williams and Arthur Miller, but to Samuel Beckett as well. Columbia Records recorded the entire performance six months into its run, an unprecedented achievement. The play won five Tony Awards, including Best Play, Best Actor, Best Actress, Best Supporting Actress, and Best Direction. The New York Drama Critics also cited it as Best Play of the 1962–1963 theater season. But when it failed to win the Pulitzer Prize—the result, many thought, of its crass, often vulgar language, two of the advisory board members resigned. It's possibly the biggest mistake the Pulitzer Prize committee has ever made. The play repeated its success the following year when Uta Hagen and Arthur Hill opened on the West End of London. Franco Zeffirelli directed the acclaimed Paris and Rome productions. And to this very day many consider *Who's Afraid of Virginia Woolf?* in the same league as two other seminal works of the American stage, *A Streetcar Named Desire* and *Long Day's Journey into Night.*

Yet for all its fame and notoriety, most people were caught off guard when Jack Warner acquired the film rights in 1964. Did anyone really want to spend three hours with four people in one house at their neighborhood movie theater, especially when all four virtually tell one another to go screw themselves?

Warner immediately assigned the producing chores and screen adaptation duties to Ernest Lehman. Lehman's credentials were—and still are—very impressive; at that time, he had already adapted to the screen *The King and I, West Side Story,* and *The Sound of Music,* as well as penning two original masterpieces, *The Sweet Smell of Success* and the ultimate Alfred Hitchcock "man on the run" thriller *North by Northwest.*

Warner's original choice for director was one of the world's most highly respected filmmakers, Fred Zinnemann. Zinnemann had already won an Oscar for directing the powerful screen version of James Jones's *From Here to Eternity* (1953), and had received four additional nominations for *The Search* (1948), *High Noon* (1952), *The Nun's Story* (1959), and *The Sundowners* (1960). Zinnemann was certainly a prestigious choice but, in hindsight, an odd one. His austere, often slow-tempo style seem incongruous for the kinds of theatrical fireworks *Who's Afraid of Virginia Woolf?* demanded. And, ultimately, Zinnemann realized this and withdrew from the project, electing instead to film the New York and London stage hit *A Man for All Seasons*. The search for the right director continued.

Meanwhile Lehman concentrated on finding actors to film the two parts of a lifetime, George and Martha. The first two thought of for the roles were Ingrid Bergman and Cary Grant. These two had worked together most memorably in Alfred Hitchcock's *Notorious* (1946). Bergman certainly had the stature as an actress to play Martha. But Martha was a loudmouthed *American* house frau. How to explain a Martha with Bergman's Swedish accent? There was also the problem of expecting an audience to accept Cary Grant, with his Cockney accent, as a realistic George. Fortunately Grant was shrewd enough to know just which parts to play and which to turn down. No matter how terrific a role George was, Grant recognized that it was not what his audience expected of him. He therefore turned down the offer. Bergman also soured on the idea, particularly after playing a mean-spirited, powerful woman in the screen adaptation of *The Visit* (1964) with Anthony Quinn, which failed miserably at the box office.

The search for both a cast and director continued. Upon Jack Warner's announcement to film *Virginia Woolf,* the press contacted Edward Albee, asking him who he wanted for the parts of George and Martha. Albee was emphatic about having James

Mason play George and Bette Davis or Ava Gardner as Martha. These were fairly inspired choices, but they were never seriously considered by Warner. Mason had been brilliant as Humbert Humbert in *Lolita* (1962), but the film was considered a disaster at the time of its release and, therefore, considered a minus as a major film draw. Bette Davis had made another of her spectacular film comebacks in 1962 with the Warner Bros. film *What Ever Happened to Baby Jane?*, but Jack Warner was not too keen on using the actress he had so bitterly fought with in the past. Besides, he felt these stars weren't strong enough to pull in the large audience the studio counted on for the film version.

The next two pairs of actors considered were Jack Lemmon and Patricia Neal for George and Martha and Warren Beatty and Pamela Tiffin supporting as Nick and Honey. At that time, Jack Lemmon was one of the most popular American actors around. He had won a supporting Oscar for *Mister Roberts* (1955) and had proven himself an impressive dramatic actor in his Oscar-nominated performance in *The Days of Wine and Roses* (1962). Patricia Neal had just won an Oscar for Best Actress as the housekeeper in *Hud* (1963), so her star was shining brightly. Warren Beatty had made a wonderful debut performance in *Splendor in the Grass* (1961) but had followed it up with a string of offbeat performances in odd films such as *Lilith* (1964), *The Roman Spring of Mrs. Stone* (1961), and *Mickey One* (1965). But he was ideally suited for the part of Nick. Pamela Tiffin was a beautiful young actress with a limited acting range, although she had played "dumb" quite expertly in Billy Wilder's cold war comedy *One, Two, Three* (1961). Miss Tiffin's career could have used a punch like *Virginia Woolf*, but it might have proven fatal for the project had she actually played the role. At the same time, Connie Stevens, then under contract to Warners, began personally to campaign for the role of Honey, but fortunately she lost the campaign. Jim Hutton also began to wage his own strategy to land the role

Jack Lemmon was one of the first stars Jack Warner wanted for the role of George.

of Nick, but Jack Warner didn't feel he was a potent enough draw for so important a part. Jack Lemmon eventually turned down the role of George (some say because Warner was unwilling to pay his asking price) and went on to make *Under the Yum Yum Tree* (1963) and *Good Neighbor Sam* (1964), two mediocre comedies that Lemmon hated but which placed him solidly as America's most popular actor. Patricia Neal ultimately turned down the role of Martha, opting instead to appear in *The Graduate*—the first feature film to be directed by Broadway's newest

James Mason was playwright Edward Albee's first choice for George. Albee wanted Bette Davis to play Martha.

star director, Mike Nichols—in the role of Mrs. Robinson. Unfortunately Miss Neal suffered a stroke in 1965, which prevented her from playing Mrs. Robinson, and it would be two years before she could work again. Mr. Beatty turned his attention to actress Leslie Caron, and the two made a fiery comedy called *Promise Her Anything,* which unfortunately failed to ignite. Beatty then went on to produce and star in a gangster film for Warner Bros. called *Bonnie and Clyde* (1967), and it was this film that solidified his career as an actor and made him a very rich man in the bargain.

Once again Bette Davis began to plead with Jack Warner to give her and Henry Fonda the roles in *Virginia Woolf.* Davis was convinced Martha would make her the first three-time Academy Award winner. But she met with the very strong objections of Ernest Lehman, who had a much more ambitious idea in mind. Whom do you get for the greatest woman's part in the last twenty years? According to Ernest Lehman, you hire the biggest actress in the world, who at that point in time happened to be Miss Elizabeth Taylor. The fact that she was nearly twenty years too young for the role did not bother Lehman, or Warner, who immediately went for the idea and quickly submitted the script for Miss Taylor's approval. Urged on by her newly wed fifth husband, actor Richard Burton, Elizabeth Taylor accepted the role of Martha, and the casting coup made front-page news across the country.

It's nearly impossible for someone who wasn't around in 1965 to comprehend the magnitude of Elizabeth Taylor's fame at that time. With her fairy-tale beauty, Taylor generated a screen charisma that had granted her stardom at the age of twelve when she appeared in *National Velvet* (1944). From that point on, M-G-M groomed Taylor into one of the biggest movie stars ever. The studio's publicity campaign orchestrated the public's fascination for her both on and off the screen. In 1951, at the ripe old age of nineteen, Taylor married hotel heir Nicky Hilton and proved herself a serious actress under George Stevens's stern direction in his Oscar-winning adaptation of Theodore Dreiser's classic *An American Tragedy,* retitled *A Place in the Sun.* As Angela Vickers, the rich girlfriend of Montgomery Clift, Elizabeth Taylor became the dream girl of every red-blooded American male in the country. This she followed up with a string of successful but inferior films, indifferent screen performances, a new marriage to actor Michael Wilding, two sons, and yet a third marriage to producer extraordinaire Michael Todd.

In 1956 Taylor again worked for Stevens, in his mammoth production of Edna Ferber's western epic *Giant,* and she made screen history along with Rock Hudson and James Dean. *Giant* is a great American film, and Taylor more than handled herself in the part, which had her age over twenty years. After *Giant* she made *Raintree County* (1957), *Cat on a Hot Tin Roof* (1958), *Suddenly, Last Summer* (1959), and *Butterfield 8* (1960). She was nominated for all four performances and won for *Butterfield 8*, the least deserving of the four. Privately she had endured tragedy with the death of Mike Todd in a plane crash, a near-fatal bout with pneumonia, and a scandalous marriage to Eddie Fisher, who had been Todd's best friend and was also the husband of her close friend Debbie Reynolds.

In 1962 Taylor became the highest-paid actress in the world when Fox offered her $1 million to replace Joan Collins as the famed queen of Egypt in the studio's production of *Cleopatra*. Taylor would eventually earn close to $7 million for *Cleopatra* after overages and profit participation. It was on the set of *Cleopatra* that her affair with her much married costar, Richard Burton, made headlines around the world. They became the most famous couple since Laurence Olivier and Vivien Leigh. Two years later they were married, after having made two more films together, *The V.I.P.s* (1963) and *The Sandpiper* (1965). Burton was slowly building his own reputation as one of screen's finest actors when he appeared in *Becket* (1964), *The Night of the Iguana* (1964), and *The Spy Who Came in from the Cold* (1965). He was nominated for Academy Awards for two of the three, and Elizabeth Taylor had not appeared in any of them. In truth, Taylor was the bigger star, but Burton was much more respected as an actor than she was. Still, in 1964, when Burton appeared in *Hamlet* on Broadway, police had to keep back the crowds every night when Taylor picked up her husband at the stage door. Their every move was reported and made front-page news. Having Elizabeth Taylor say yes to Martha was an enormous asset in Lehman's and Warner's eyes, regardless of any potential drawbacks in her performance of the role.

While Lehman kept looking for the right director, he met with his star at her bungalow at the Beverly Hills Hotel to discuss possible costars for the role of George. Richard Burton was sitting alongside Taylor on a couch while Lehman went over a list of possible candidates—in fact, quite a few candidates, but none of them Richard Burton. Finally Taylor stopped Lehman and with her characteristic aplomb hitched her thumb toward her husband, and said, "Hey, how about him?" Lehman quickly realized that what Miss Taylor wanted she was going to get, so he offered Burton the part of George—and was accepted. When the announcement was made, Edward Albee, who was not happy with the casting, suggested they get Debbie Reynolds and Eddie Fisher as Nick and Honey. His suggestion was ignored.

It was the Burtons who championed Mike Nichols as director for *Who's Afraid of Virginia Woolf?* Mike Nichols had befriended the Burtons, having met Richard Burton during his run on Broadway in the Lerner and Loewe musical *Camelot.* Nichols and his partner, Elaine May, had been considered among the brightest comic talents of the fifties. After they split up in the early sixties, Nichols directed four hit plays in a row, all in one year: *Barefoot in the Park, Luv, The Knack,* and *The Odd Couple.* He won two Tony Awards for Best Direction, and Joseph E. Levine subsequently signed him to make his film debut as director of *The Graduate.* The Burtons were convinced that although Nichols lacked experience as a screen director, he was brilliant theatrically. They needed someone to capture the characterizations and, more important, the sardonic humor of the play. Instinctively they felt Nichols would bring a freshness and an energy that could make *Who's Afraid of Virginia Woolf?* the greatest film of their respective careers. With some strong-arming from Jack Warner and the loss of Patricia Neal as Mrs. Robinson, Joseph E. Levine agreed to postpone *The Graduate* and allow *Virginia Woolf* to be Nichols's first film. Levine realized

Bette Davis begged Jack Warner for the role of Martha, thinking it would win her a third Academy Award.

that if *Virginia Woolf* was the smash he felt it might be, then he could cash in on its success by touting Nichols as his prize property for *The Graduate*. Besides, if Nichols needed to practice on a first film, let it be one for Jack Warner. That way he'd be seasoned when he worked on *The Graduate*.

For the roles of Nick and Honey, Nichols and Lehman looked to Broadway. Nichols desperately wanted the young Robert Redford for the part of Nick. He had recently directed him in the comedy smash *Barefoot in the Park,* where Redford had achieved instant matinee idol status. Initially, Redford was interested. But he changed his mind when he was offered the lead role opposite Natalie Wood in *This Property Is Condemned,* based on a one-act by Tennessee Williams. George Segal, a rising young actor who had appeared in *Ship of Fools* (1965) and *King Rat* (1965), was ultimately cast as Nick. For the part of Honey, Nichols engaged the brightest new comic actress on Broadway, Sandy Dennis, whose performance in *Any Wednesday* had earned her raves and a Tony Award. Casting her proved to be nothing less than inspired.

When filming began in July of 1965 at Smith College in Northampton, Massachusetts, Elizabeth Taylor had gained twenty pounds, weighing in at 155, and had completely deglamorized her famous beauty. Burton looked seedy and gray, although he was not quite forty when filming began. The shooting lasted until December, with the interiors shot in Los Angeles at the Warners lot. Nichols demanded more of Taylor than any other director had. Frequently she complained over his relentless insistence on redoing scene after scene. But with Burton's coaching, she delivered. In fact, by the time the film completed shooting, Elizabeth Taylor and Richard Burton had become George and Martha offscreen as well.

Upon seeing a rough cut of the film, Burton was supposedly disappointed by his performance as George, finding it ''indifferent.'' But he, along with everyone else, was quite astonished

In her first major screen role, Broadway star Sandy Dennis won an Oscar for her performance as Honey.

with Elizabeth Taylor. It was the part of a lifetime, and she had made the most of it.

In June of 1966 *Time* magazine heralded the arrival of a classic. *Who's Afraid of Virginia Woolf?* had arrived on screen with all its teeth. No other American film had treated sexual politics so frankly and with such language. In many ways, *Who's Afraid of Virginia Woolf?* broke new ground for American films and was the forerunner for the American New Wave of 1967. Elizabeth Taylor and Richard Burton were hailed as the screen's greatest acting team. And when the film opened, it was hailed unanimously as a masterpiece. Never again would Miss Taylor be considered second to her husband in the acting department. The film played through the rest of the year and was an unqualified hit, even though it retained a strict "no one under sixteen allowed" policy.

The following February, *Who's Afraid of Virginia Woolf?* was nominated for thirteen Academy Awards. (The film's nearest competition was *A Man for All Seasons,* with a total of ten Oscar nominations.) The entire cast was nominated—a first in academy history. Mike Nichols, who was of course nominated, had become the hottest director in town, much to Joseph E. Levine's delight.

On Oscar night Miss Taylor was a no-show, saying she couldn't leave her husband alone in Paris. *Virginia Woolf* won five Oscars, including Best Supporting Actress for Sandy Dennis and Best Actress for Elizabeth Taylor. Fred Zinnemann, the film's first-choice director, won over Mike Nichols for *A Man for All Seasons,* and Paul Scofield, repeating his stage performance as Sir Thomas More in *A Man for All Seasons,* won as Best Actor over Richard Burton. In retrospect, it is hard to understand how Burton was passed over. Scofield is superb as Thomas More, but Burton, as George, showed the "real fire" great actors generate from within. His performance is nothing less than spectacular. Burton would be nominated seven times for an Oscar but was never a winner. Scofield preferred stage to film and spent the rest of his career primarily on the West End of London.

Elizabeth Taylor and Richard Burton reached their peak in *Who's Afraid of Virginia Woolf?* Neither ever gave stronger performances, and in the end both will probably be best remembered as George and Martha. Their marriage ended in 1974, with each blaming George and Martha for its eventual demise. The actors had become too much like their parts, and their private life had come to resemble an off-screen *Who's Afraid of Virginia Woolf?* The film forever changed their lives. Never again would Elizabeth Taylor be considered anything less than a wonderful actress, and *Woolf?* helped solidify Burton's movie star status. Today the film stands as an American landmark, its quality and brilliance a testament to the cinematic heights this country can reach.

CASABLANCA (1943)

Sometimes a film's success is determined strictly in terms of "casting chemistry," that magical spark between an actor and actress that can elevate a film all by itself. Such could be said for Frank Capra's *It Happened One Night* (1934), with Clark Gable and Claudette Colbert; *The Thin Man* (1934), starring William Powell and Myrna Loy; *The Awful Truth* (1937), pairing Cary Grant with Irene Dunne; and all of the Fred Astaire–Ginger Rogers musicals. Sometimes a film's success is serendipitous or the result of timing, capturing and capitalizing on the feelings of a nation. Certainly this was true in 1979, when James Bridges's suspense thriller about nuclear waste plants, *The China Syndrome* opened and two weeks later the Three Mile Island accident occurred. Suddenly *The China Syndrome* was front-page news across the world and reaped the benefits of "good timing."

Then there are the films that have the good fortune to be blessed with both casting chemistry *and* topicality. And no other film hit a bigger grand slam on both accounts than Warner

Bros.' classic contemporary love story of 1943, *Casablanca,* produced by Hall Wallis. The chance encounter of two former lovers in a bar in Nazi-occupied Casablanca was as much a part of the American experience during World War II as the Battle of the Bulge. As the former lovers Rick and Ilsa, Humphrey Bogart and Ingrid Bergman achieved screen immortality; they will always be best remembered for *Casablanca.* The film's theme song, "As Time Goes By," became a classic, even though it had been indifferently received when it was first written, eleven years earlier.

Casablanca was rushed into prerelease at the Hollywood

Three superb reasons for the continuing popularity of Casablanca, *from left to right, Paul Henreid, Ingrid Bergman, and Claude Rains.*

Theatre in New York City on November 26, 1942, in order to take advantage of the recent Allied recapture of Casablanca from the Nazis. And Warners milked its topicality "to the max," making it a "must see" film upon its wide release in January of 1943. Needless to say, it was wildly successful, and the public's love affair continues uninterrupted to this day. With the possible exceptions of *Gone With the Wind* and *The Wizard of Oz,* no other American film is as cherished as *Casablanca,* if not by the critics, then most assuredly by the public. And although it's impossible to envision *Casablanca* with anyone but Bogart and Bergman in the two lead romantic roles, in the beginning they were not even in the running.

The origin of *Casablanca* was relatively modest. An unproduced play by Murray Burnett and Joan Alison called *Everybody Comes to Rick's* arrived at Warner Bros. the day after the Japanese attacked Pearl Harbor. A studio reader, Stephen Karnot, thought it "a box office natural—for Bogart, or Cagney, or Raft in out-of-the-usual roles, and perhaps Mary Astor." Then Irene Lee, head of the studio's story department, took the property to Hal Wallis, who ran production at Warners for Jack Warner, and insisted he buy it—which he did, for $20,000. From that point on, Hal Wallis was to take full credit for the success of *Casablanca,* while Jack Warner would do likewise. The writing team of Julius and Philip Epstein was assigned to write the first draft, with (according to Wallis) Bogart in mind as the main character, Rick. Thus the brothers began, using much of the original play as source material—although later on they and Howard Koch, who was brought in to do a rewrite, claimed to have invented all of *Casablanca.* The screenplay was still incomplete when shooting began and was constantly being written during the actual shooting. This caused tension on the set, since the actors never quite knew what would be expected of them each day.

Ingrid Bergman and Humphrey Bogart in Casablanca.

Before Wallis set Bogart for the part of Rick, one memo from Jack Warner confirms his desire to see George Raft play the role. Raft was the perfect prototype for Rick, hard-boiled, desperate, but ultimately a "good guy." And Raft had made Jack Warner millions during the thirties. But Raft's judgment had been poor when, in the early forties, he turned down a number of roles that might have salvaged his fading career. Perhaps the biggest mistake he made was in turning down the part of Sam Spade in John Huston's 1941 remake of Dashiell Hammett's *The Maltese Falcon*. A Warner Bros. contract player who had been working steadily for five years inherited the part and, as Sam Spade, became the studio's hottest new leading man. His name was Humphrey Bogart.

Bogart had made an impression on the New York stage in Robert Sherwood's *The Petrified Forest*, in 1935. When the

Warner Bros. film version was being cast, Leslie Howard was asked to reprieve his Broadway performance. Howard said he would only if Bogart was cast as well, along with Bette Davis. The studio agreed, and Bogart was a hit in the film version. But the actor, who was immediately put under a seven-year contract to the studio, proved problematic, with his less-than-glamorous looks and his somewhat peculiar attitude. Bogart was tough, but he was too good to be used just in villainous roles. He played opposite Bette Davis in *Marked Woman* (1937) and *Dark Victory* (1939), and although audiences liked him, he did not catch on. Then came Sam Spade, and Bogart was made. The hard-boiled but likable persona melded superbly with the hard-nosed, sexy private eye. Suddenly Bogart was a sex symbol. After *The Maltese Falcon,* Bogart inherited another role rejected by George Raft: *High Sierra,* directed by Raoul Walsh. This was one of the first film noir classics of the forties, a genre Bogart's personality completely captured. The film, with Bogart as a killer on the lam with love interest Ida Lupino, went through the roof at the box office.

Thus it seems fitting to imagine that the role of Rick in *Casablanca* fell to Bogart only because, once again, George Raft turned down the opportunity. In this case, however, the second-choice casting resulted in a performance that turned Bogart into the biggest male actor in Hollywood. (Still another item that countered Wallis's intention to cast Bogart as Rick Blaine was the studio's own press release announcing contract players Ronald Reagan and Ann Sheridan as the leads. There's no other proof that Ronald Reagan was seriously considered for the part of Rick, so the press release might have been the brainchild of an overly zealous publicist.)

In their screen adaptation, the Epsteins depicted both Rick and his former lady love as Americans. Therefore it's obvious that at the start no one thought of Ingrid Bergman as the female lead. The first actress under serious consideration was Ann

Sheridan, one of the studio's most popular contract players. In fact, Hall Wallis confirmed this casting of Bogart and Sheridan to Warner as a done deal, yet less than a week later he was negotiating with M-G-M to loan out Hedy Lamarr for the role. Within a week Rick's former lover Lois had become Rick's former lover Ilsa, and Ann Sheridan was no longer in *Casablanca*.

Mayer refused to loan out Lamarr to Warners, so Wallis next considered Michèle Morgan, whom he tested in April of 1942. But her poor English and her high asking price disillusioned him. Besides, a brighter star looked as though she might be available for the role, a natural for the part named Ingrid Bergman.

In 1939 David O. Selznick had introduced two actresses to the American public. The more publicized of the two was Vivien Leigh, who was playing Scarlet O'Hara in Selznick's epic *Gone With the Wind*. The other actress was a Swedish import, a young, fresh talent who was repeating her performance in the Swedish film that initially attracted Selznick to her. Called *Intermezzo,* it costarred Leslie Howard. *Intermezzo* proved very popular to the audiences of 1939, and Ingrid Bergman became a hot commodity for Selznick. He immediately loaned her out for an outrageous price to M-G-M, where Bergman made her reputation in *Adam Had Four Sons* (1941) and particularly in *Dr. Jekyll and Mr. Hyde* (1942), with Spencer Tracy and Lana Turner, directed by *Gone With the Wind*'s Victor Fleming. Next she campaigned successfully for the role of Maria in Paramount's screen version of Ernest Hemingway's best-selling 1940 novel *For Whom the Bell Tolls,* opposite Gary Cooper.

Ingrid Bergman was definitely a star on the rise, but in the fall/winter of 1941–1942, the talented young actress found herself in Rochester, New York, where her husband, Peter Lindstrom, was studying to become a neurosurgeon. Bergman was sick of life in Rochester, even if it meant spending more time with her three-year-old daughter, Pia. She was desperate to return to work, afraid she was losing the momentum her career had gained. Therefore, when Wallis contacted her with the offer to play Ilsa, she jumped at the chance. After a very heavy negotiating session with Selznick to loan out his Ingrid to Warner Bros., Wallis was able to announce to the press that *Casablanca* would star Humphrey Bogart and Ingrid Bergman.

For the third lead, that of Ilsa's Resistance-leading husband-hero, Victor Laszlo, Hal Wallis's first choice was Dutch actor Philip Dorn, but Dorn was committed to *Random Harvest* at M-G-M at the same time, so he was forced to refuse. Next Wallis tried Jean-Pierre Aumont, then an unknown young French actor, but Warner wanted someone more important. Joseph Cotten, Dean Jagger, and Herbert Marshall were all considered, but ultimately the role was offered to Paul Henreid, who initially turned it down but finally accepted when he was assured of equal billing alongside Bogart and Bergman. Henreid had created quite a romantic sensation the year before when he'd costarred with Bette Davis in one of the greatest Cinderella soap operas ever filmed, *Now, Voyager* (1941).

The rest of the cast included such established character actors as Conrad Veidt, Sydney Greenstreet, Peter Lorre, Dooley Wilson, S. Z. Sakall, and the fabulous Claude Rains. As the evil Nazi major, Conrad Veidt had won out over Otto Preminger, and although Clarence Muse was the first choice as the piano-playing Sam, Dooley Wilson finally ended up playing it.

Filming began in July of 1942 at Van Nuys Airport and later on the Warner Bros. sound stages under Michael Curtiz's direction. Curtiz had not been Wallis's initial choice—William Wyler had. But Wyler had refused the job, having just made his own World War II film, *Mrs. Miniver* (1942), for M-G-M Curtiz was the favorite director on the Warners lot, responsible for such past hits as *The Charge of the Light Brigade* (1936), *The Adventures of Robin Hood* (1938), *Four Daughters* (1938), and *Yankee Doodle Dandy* (1942).

Shooting proceeded in the actual order seen in the film,

One of the original posters for the 1943 Oscar-winning Best Picture.

mostly because the script was not yet finished. Everyone was in somewhat of a daze throughout the filming since no one knew how the film would eventually turn out. Meanwhile Bogart's third wife, actress Mayo Methot, was badgering cast members on the set every day, convinced her husband was having an affair with Bergman, which he was not. Dooley Wilson didn't know how to play the piano, so he faked his keyboard rendition of "As Time Goes By." And the cast shot the last scenes of the film in no more than one take. Upon completion, everyone left—tired and unaware of the masterpiece they'd created.

Casablanca proved to be the biggest hit of 1943 and the most profitable film for Warner Bros. that year. The critics and public were equally enthusiastic. Humphrey Bogart became the biggest male star in the country. Ingrid Bergman received her share of acclaim, and with the release of *For Whom the Bell Tolls* later on in the year, she became the biggest female draw in the country. Claude Rains nearly stole the film, and "As Time Goes By" was the biggest single recording of the year.

Casablanca was nominated by the academy for Best Picture, Best Actor, Best Supporting Actor (Claude Rains), Best Director, and Best Screenplay; it won three awards—Best Picture, Best Director, and Best Screenplay. Ingrid Bergman was nominated for Best Actress for *For Whom the Bell Tolls*.

Casablanca is as popular today as it was in 1943. Much of its dialogue has become immortalized as part of the popular vocabulary ("Here's looking at you, kid," "Round up the usual suspects," and, most famous of all, "Play it, Sam"). Most of all, it's hard to imagine the film without Bogart and Bergman. Their casting chemistry in this classic wartime film brightened a dark period in our history with a much needed ray of romance and hope.

One of the savviest strategies ever employed by Hollywood's original production boy wonder, Irving Thalberg, began with his recognition of character actor Lon Chaney's immense genius. It was during his tenure at Universal Pictures that Thalberg quickly realized and understood the way Chaney's grotesque impersonations could convincingly frighten audiences and the potential box office revenues this sort of gift might generate for the studio. He instantly signed this master of the macabre to a studio contract.

Their first collaboration was a lavish screen rendition of Victor Hugo's popular novel *Notre Dame de Paris,* more commonly known as *The Hunchback of Notre Dame.* Under Thalberg's close supervision, director Wallace Worsley managed to sustain a reasonable balance between the epic and the horror of this fifteenth-century "Beauty and the Beast" tale of religious hypocrisy and social corruption. As Quasimodo, the tragically deformed bellringer of Notre Dame, Chaney was both physically and emotionally brilliant. Initially audiences were repelled

Boris Karloff was immortalized by his role as the monster in Frankenstein.

by Chaney's ghoulish appearance, but his heartbreaking compassion in his unrequited love for the beautiful gypsy dancer Esmeralda won our hearts. The 1923 silent release was nothing less than a sensation, contributing handsomely to Universal's balance sheets. Within a year young Thalberg left the studio for the newly formed Metro-Goldwyn-Mayer under Louis B. Mayer's leadership, but Chaney, now an established film star favorite, remained at Universal Pictures, starring in a string of very successful horror films and thrillers. His bizarre screen characterizations quickly familiarized him to audiences as the "Man of a Thousand Faces." Universal Pictures increased the number of horror movies on its upcoming production schedules and soon established itself as the home of the horror genre.

All in all, 1925 proved a remarkable year for both Lon Chaney and Irving Thalberg. At Universal, Chaney reached the apex of his film career, playing the title role in Gaston Leroux's nineteenth-century Gothic melodrama *The Phantom of the Opera*. As the mad phantom of the Paris Opera House, Lon Chaney offered one of the greatest interpretations in cinema history. Under Rupert Julian's embellished direction, the actor terrorized film audiences, making *The Phantom of the Opera* the second most successful film of 1925. The *most* successful film of the year was one of Irving Thalberg's projects for M-G-M, the extraordinary World War I epic *The Big Parade*. Acclaimed a masterpiece, the largest "event" film since *Birth of a Nation* ten years before, *The Big Parade* broke all box office records up until that time, made a star of John Gilbert (under King Vidor's masterful direction), and secured Metro-Goldwyn-Mayer's position as a prestige studio—an honor that would evade Universal for nearly half a century.

Lon Chaney moved to Metro-Goldwyn-Mayer and worked for Thalberg until his untimely death in 1930 at the age of forty-seven. By this time Thalberg's sound judgment on what the public wanted to see had made Metro-Goldwyn-Mayer the most popular fiefdom in Hollywood. The studio turned out quality films along with B-movie programmers and had under contract the most impressive roster of talent in the world.

Universal Pictures, meanwhile, continued successfully to produce B-grade programmers, striking "prestige" only once, with the 1930 Academy Award–winning production of Erich Maria Remarque's antiwar classic *All Quiet on the Western Front,* directed by Lewis Milestone and starring a very youthful Lew Ayres. The next year, the studio hit pay dirt with its production of *Dracula,* based on Bram Stoker's best-selling vampire thriller.

Based on the successful 1927 stage adaptation, and directed by Tod Browning (the stylishly perverse auteur of the then unreleasable M-G-M horror flick *(Freaks), Dracula* starred Bela Lugosi, the Hungarian-born actor who had played the bloodsucking count for nearly three years on Broadway. Movie audiences loved both the film and Lugosi. *Dracula* spawned more offspring than the old lady who lived in a shoe. Afterward Lugosi found himself enshrined—or imprisoned—in the horror genre and rarely ventured beyond its boundaries. But *Dracula* in no way prepared audiences for what Universal would offer the following year.

In 1932 the studio released James Whale's very Germanic production of Mary Shelley's Gothic classic *Frankenstein, or Prometheus Unbound.* Originally Bela Lugosi was offered the role of the monster created from dead body parts by Dr. Frankenstein, but the amount of makeup required for the part made Lugosi uncomfortable, and he found the script unexciting. Next to be approached was a very young actor with little experience, John Carradine, but he too turned down the role. Finally, a British character actor, Boris Karloff, said yes, and a legend was born. Leslie Howard was hotly sought for the title role, but he found the entire undertaking undignified. Colin Clive played Victor Frankenstein, a role he would undertake six more times. A relatively unknown Bette Davis was first choice for the female lead, but the studio wanted someone a bit more familiar, so Mae Clarke was selected. (Clarke had made a name for herself in *Public Enemy,* when James Cagney shoved a grapefruit in her face.)

Today *Frankenstein* is a camp classic, but in 1932 moviegoers found it no laughing matter. They were too damned scared even to think about laughing. *Frankenstein* proved to be an even bigger gold mine for Universal than *Dracula.* And the studio continued to exploit that mine for the next twenty years. The most memorable *Frankenstein* sequel was the 1935 *Bride of Frankenstein,* once again with Boris Karloff and and Elsa Lanchester as his hissing bride. *Bride* was actually superior to the original film.

Eventually Universal Pictures became known as "the House of Horror." The studio turned out films teeming with vampires and manmade monsters; unearthed mummies on nasty, spiteful missions of revenge; introduced nervous young men who, by day, were in a state of spiritual turmoil for turning into werewolves the night before. These B pictures kept the studio in the black, although by the 1950s both Dracula and Frankenstein had become bloodless, lifeless caricatures, sharing equal billing with the studio's leading comedy team, Bud Abbott and Lou Costello. Some of the major studios, particularly Warner Bros. with *House of Wax* (1953) and *Murders in the Rue Morgue* (1954), ventured into horror, but none took it seriously. The films were profitable, but they were hardly respectable, and in the end the other studios were content to allow Universal full reign of that dubious genre.

Then, by the mid-fifties, a third-rate film production company, American International, began producing horror films aimed directly at the rapidly growing teenage audiences. Many of the pictures were produced by an ambitious young newcomer named Roger Corman, on budgets smaller than Jack Warner's weekly grocery bill. In 1957 the company produced *I Was a Teen-age Werewolf,* starring Michael Landon, and *I Was a*

Teenage Frankenstein. Both films went right through the roof, making back over a hundred times their cost. Suddenly schlock master director William Castle appeared with *The House on Haunted Hill* (1958) and *The Tingler* (1959), both featuring Vincent Price. Audiences swarmed to them. Afterward came the release of several films—most featuring the now perennial Vincent Price—based very loosely indeed on the works of Edgar Allan Poe, starting in 1960 with *The House of Usher.* They were hardly great works of art, but Hollywood could not fail to notice the enormous returns they made on their original investments.

One man in particular took great interest and by doing so forever changed the horror genre. His name was Alfred Hitchcock.

Alfred Hitchcock has long been acknowledged as "a pantheon director," to borrow a phrase from film critic Andrew Sarris. Indeed, Hitchcock's name above the title was as potent a box office force as any movie star's. To the general public he was affectionately known as "the master of suspense." For film buffs and historians, he meant much more than that. Along with D. W. Griffith, Sergei Eisenstein, and Fritz Lang, Hitchcock created the very grammar of filmmaking, mastering montage and handling movement in scenes in a manner so original and significative that his movies were instantly recognizable as such to audiences all over the world.

Hitchcock, a former production designer, was greatly influenced by the silent German Expressionist movies of the 1920s. His first film, a silent entitled *The Lodger* (1926), was a moody, suspenseful retelling of the Jack the Ripper atrocities. From then on Hitchcock quickly became England's most innovative and financially successful film director. His films perfectly blended unbearable suspense with a wry sense of humor. During his British period, "Hitch" created two masterpieces that

Alfred Hitchcock elevated the horror genre with his classic Psycho.

brought him worldwide attention—*The 39 Steps* (1935) and *The Lady Vanishes* (1938).

In 1939, as Britain went to war, Hitchcock came to Hollywood under contract to one of the town's leading producers, David O. Selznick. No two men could have been farther apart in their expectations of a working relationship. Hitchcock demanded total control of his films, with no outside interference from either studios or producers. Selznick was the most hands-on producer in town, issuing memos that at times rivaled Tolstoy in length. Yet somehow or other the combination worked, and their first effort, *Rebecca,* based on the marvelous novel by Daphne du Maurier, won an Oscar for Best Picture of 1940.

Hitchcock continued making American films, returning only occasionally to England. He became an American citizen during the 1940s, when his films dominated the cinema. One gem followed another: *Foreign Correspondent* in 1940; *Shadow of a Doubt* in 1943, written by Sally Benson and Thornton Wilder; *Lifeboat* in 1944, written by John Steinbeck and starring Tallulah Bankhead; *Spellbound* in 1945 and *Notorious* in 1946, both of which were written by Ben Hecht and starred Ingrid Bergman. Hitch was not as successful with the films he directed in the latter part of the forties, but they remained profitable all the same.

Then, in 1951 he returned with a grand-slam thriller called *Strangers on a Train* and with this film entered his golden period. Hitchcock's American films of the 1950s made use of the finest talent in Hollywood—Cary Grant, James Stewart, Montgomery Clift, Henry Fonda, Doris Day, Eva Marie Saint—and were exceptionally well received by the public and, for the most part, the critics as well. In 1955 he created a weekly television series, "Alfred Hitchcock Presents," which ran for nine seasons and today is shown daily in syndication. Hitch introduced each new show, so his rotund profile and droll speaking voice became cozily familiar to audiences. He took a promising young Grace Kelly and transformed her into the bewitching sophisticated screen persona she later adapted for the performance of her life, as princess of Monaco. Their three films together—*Dial M for Murder* (1954), *Rear Window* (1954), and *To Catch a Thief* (1955)—turned Grace Kelly into a major movie star. In 1956 Hitchcock redid his own *The Man Who Knew Too Much* with James Stewart, creating a second version far superior to the original. In 1958 he made what he thought to be his masterpiece, *Vertigo,* starring James Stewart and Kim Novak (who was a last-minute replacement for a pregnant Vera Miles). The film was slammed critically and was pulled out of distribution by Paramount after only three weeks in theaters. Ironically, today, whenever a "ten best films of all time" list appears, *Vertigo* is

Vincent Price had a long prosperous career in a string of horror films during the forties, fifties, sixties, and seventies.

generally included and is often called Hitchcock's best movie. The "master of suspense" then finished out the decade with a film that epitomized the "wrong man on the run" theme he had explored since *The 39 Steps*. Called *North by Northwest*, the picture featured one of Cary Grant's best performances and was hugely successful.

But as the decade ended, Hitchcock wasn't capitalizing on his reputation by planning a blockbuster project. In fact, he was making a low-budget horror film such as the kind American International favored—using his television crew and shooting on a six-week schedule in utter secrecy. The movie, based on a

One of Hollywood's best and most sophisticated couples, Cary Grant and Grace Kelly in Hitchcock's To Catch a Thief.

minor thriller by Robert Bloch, was called *Psycho,* and to this day it is considered by many to be the most terrifying film of all time.

Suggested by the actual grotesque 1957 Ed Gein murders on his isolated Wisconsin farm, *Psycho* is the tale of a likable but lonely young man, Norman Bates, who runs a failing motel and lives right behind in a spooky Victorian mansion with his "sick old mother," who, it seems, is also a homicidal maniac. Late one night he registers a guest, an attractive young woman named Marion Crane, who is on the run after stealing forty thousand dollars. She has a simple supper with Norman and then retires to her room; there, while showering, she's promptly and viciously stabbed to death by Mrs. Bates, Norman's mother. In order to protect his mother, Norman dutifully disposes of the body and the mess and hopes nothing will happen. But Mrs. Bates strikes again, this time slashing to death a snoopy private investigator. She nearly manages to do the same to Marion's sister, but Marion's boyfriend stops her, and in so doing, he—and the audience—discovers that Mrs. Bates is actually Norman in drag, psychotically convinced he is the mother he had murdered ten years before.

Anthony Perkins was the first and only choice to play the pivotal role of Norman Bates. Son of the great Broadway actor Osgood Perkins, young Tony had already made an impact on audiences, especially in his Academy Award–nominated performance as Gary Cooper's son in William Wyler's 1956 Quaker epic *Friendly Persuasion.* Perkins confessed he thought the part was a chance of a lifetime, and his prediction proved true: Perkins was forever after associated with his role in *Psycho* and would eventually reprieve the part in the less-than-memorable sequels that followed.

Casting Marion Crane, the shower murder victim, was more complicated. Hitchcock generally favored blond actresses in his starring roles. He had just finished working with Eva Marie

Saint in *North by Northwest,* so her name was naturally brought up first. But Hitchcock turned her down and went on to look at Lana Turner—who, after surviving a scandal the previous year in which her daughter had murdered Lana's lover, had just made a comeback in the soap opera *Imitation of Life.* Turner had already turned down the lead in Otto Preminger's *Anatomy of a Murder* (1959), and Lee Remick had benefited from it. But Hitchcock didn't care much for Turner and went on to look at Hope Lange and Piper Laurie. He even thought about the ever-wholesome star of *Oklahoma* and *Carousel*—Shirley Jones—but found her sweet image too sticky to deal with. Hitchcock finally decided upon Janet Leigh, a bright young graduate of Metro-Goldwyn-Mayer who had appeared mostly in costume dramas with her then husband Tony Curtis. At first Miss Leigh was hesitant to accept when she learned her character was out of the film after the first fifty minutes, but she soon realized that a good supporting role in an Alfred Hitchcock movie was better than the lead in anyone else's film.

For the role of Sam Loomis, Marion's boyfriend, a number of hunky-looking leading men were considered, including Stuart Whitman, Tom Tryon, Cliff Robertson, Leslie Nielsen, Tom Laughlin, and Robert Loggia, who would play Sam in *Psycho II* in 1983. Rod Taylor was also considered for the part, but Hitchcock went for John Gavin, the handsome leading man at Universal (Hitch would cast Rod Taylor as the lead in his follow-up to *Psycho, The Birds*). After casting Gavin, Hitchcock had major regrets and would constantly refer to him as "the wooden Indian."

Filming began in November of 1959 under a heavy veil of secrecy. No one was allowed to discuss the movie. Shooting took place on the Universal lot with a technical crew from Hitchcock's weekly TV series, all of whom knew how to work quickly. The shower sequence took over a week to film, but the rest of the film was completed in five. Janet Leigh was not used in the shower sequence; she was replaced by her stand-in, because it was the last scene to be filmed and it was a nude scene which she would not have been comfortable shooting. In fact, none of the key players were involved in that sequence. When Hitchcock completed the film and showed the rough cut to his key crew members, without the music, they seriously considered cutting it down to an hour and using it as an episode on his television series. The whole first part seemed long and drawn out. Then Hitch had his favorite composer, veteran colleague Bernard Herrmann, write the brilliant music, and *Psycho* came together. Herrmann's legendary score gave the film a suspense it otherwise lacked, particularly in the long sequence leading Marion Crane to the Bates Motel.

Psycho opened to the public in the summer of 1960 without benefit of reviews. No critics had been allowed to see the film before its opening. A strict "no one will be allowed to enter the theater after the film has begun" policy was enforced. Critics reacted with apprehension, most of them dismissive of Hitchcock's foray into the "horror genre." But the public went wild, and the film was a smash hit. Everywhere, everyone was talking about *Psycho*. People became afraid of taking showers; in fact, *Psycho* forever changed the way people would think about showering. Who hasn't had a moment of fear when getting into a shower in an empty house?

After its American premiere, *Psycho* opened in England and Europe, where it was instantly hailed as a masterpiece. Tony Perkins won the Cannes Film Festival Award for Best Actor. The French saw it, quite simply, as the most terrifying movie ever made. By the end of the year most American critics had revised their opinions, and *Psycho* turned up on almost all of the important "ten best" lists.

Psycho was nominated for four Academy Awards, including Best Director and Best Supporting Actress (Janet Leigh). But it failed to win a Best Picture nomination, losing out to an infinitely inferior achievement, *The Alamo*. (Most people blamed this on the fact that *Psycho* was viewed as a "horror film," a genre not worthy of nomination.) Bernard Herrmann's outrageously wonderful score was overlooked as well. And on Oscar night Janet Leigh lost to the wholesome Shirley Jones for Best Supporting Actress in her role as a slut in *Elmer Gantry*.

Today, *Psycho* is considered Alfred Hitchcock's masterpiece and one of the most impressive films of all time—proof that a genre is never second-rate if a first-rate talent is working on it. *Psycho* was rereleased in 1965 by Universal, who had acquired the rights from Paramount. It was fitting that this horror milestone ultimately became a property of the House of Horror. Hitchcock had produced *Psycho* for $800,000; currently, with the various rereleases and video sales and television showings, the film has generated revenues in the area of $200 million. For "the master of suspense," it clearly was a most successful accomplishment. Naturally a whole crop of "slasher" films followed *Psycho,* but none duplicated its power or its glory until nearly thirteen years later.

William Peter Blatty was first exposed to exorcism in 1949 while still a junior at Georgetown University in Washington, D.C. He had read a disturbing but fascinating account in the *Washington Post* of a fourteen-year-old Mt. Rainier boy who had been exorcised of demonic possession by a Catholic priest, with the ritual taking place in both the Washington area and St. Louis. The graphic description of demonic possession struck a strong chord in Blatty's fervent imagination and would eventually be the seedling for his shocking 1970 best-selling hit novel *The Exorcist*. Blatty by this point had been making a living as a successful screenwriter. He had even based the main character, an actress named Chris O'Neil, on his close friend, screen star Shirley MacLaine. *The Exorcist* was one of those books you could not put down. It was gloriously readable and undeniably frightening, especially the detailed account of a twelve-year-old girl's demonic possession and the battle between good and evil—Satan and an Older Priest called Father Merrin.

When Warner Bros. acquired the screen rights, many were skeptical. How could the movie depict some of the more vile moments of the novel, particularly the masturbation scene with a crucifix performed by the possessed daughter? *The Exorcist* might come to the screen, but most people felt it would be a watered down version, pale by comparison. They were wrong to think so. Blatty was hired as a producer and screenwriter. Stanley Kubrick was approached to direct and showed real interest, but Blatty was worried about the director's "all controls" policy. A list was assembled of the best possible directors, including Arthur Penn and Mike Nichols, both of whom turned it down. But Blatty had someone else in mind to realize his occult masterpiece, a young New York director not on the studio's "A" list. His name was William Friedkin.

Friedkin had directed a number of small, interesting, but relatively unsuccessful films, including an adaptation of Harold Pinter's *The Birthday Party* (1968) and *The Night They Raided Minsky's* (1968); the latter had caught the attention of Blatty, although it proved a disaster at the box office. It was unusual for Blatty to insist on a director without a sound track record, but after meeting Friedkin, he persisted, and the studio agreed. Their acquiescence was not entirely whimsical. Rumors were flying that Friedkin's latest film, a cop thriller made on a tight budget, was something unusual.

It turned out the rumors were right: William Friedkin suddenly became the hottest director in town when his film *The French Connection* ripped its way across the nation in the fall of 1971. *The French Connection* was an edge-of-your-seat thriller with the greatest chase sequence ever filmed. It made a star out of Gene Hackman, who till then had been thought of as a sup-

porting character actor. It gave an enormous push to Roy
Scheider's career and earned him one of the film's ten Academy
Award nominations the following spring. *The French Connection*
went on to win five awards, including Best Picture, Best Actor,
and Best Director. Friedkin's sleeper had made him the ideal
choice for *The Exorcist,* and Warner Bros. was elated to have already signed him on.

After Friedkin had Blatty completely revise the first draft of
the screenplay, casting commenced. Naturally, the first person
approached for the role of the actress/mother was its inspiration, Shirley MacLaine. And although MacLaine had wanted to
play the part, she wanted to start before the production was
ready to do so. In fact, MacLaine had wanted to start filming
before Friedkin had been hired. She was ready the day the
book hit the number one spot on the *New York Times* Best-Seller
List. But Blatty backed off, feeling too pressured, so MacLaine
made her own occult film, a big dud called *The Possession of Joel
Delaney* (1972).

Blatty next approached one of Hollywood's biggest and most
controversial stars, Jane Fonda. Fonda had been making films
for over a decade but was not regarded as a serious actress until

*Angst-ridden Ellen Burstyn welcomes Father Merrin, a.k.a. The Exorcist (Max
Von Sydow), to her home.*

1969, with her performance in *They Shoot Horses, Don't They?* For the part of Gloria she won her first Oscar nomination and her first New York Film Critics Award as Best Actress. This she followed up with Alan J. Pakula's thriller *Klute* (1971). For her performance as Bree Daniels, the hooker—a role turned down by Barbra Streisand—she won a second New York Film Critics Award as Best Actress and an Academy Award for Best Actress. So Blatty was anxious, as was the studio, to have Fonda in the lead. But Fonda informed Blatty that she couldn't play Chris O'Neil in *The Exorcist* because she didn't believe in magic.

William Friedkin solved the Chris O'Neil casting problem by crusading for Ellen Burstyn. Miss Burstyn was hardly a box office draw, but her stock had gone up considerably after she had been nominated for an Oscar in Peter Bogdanovich's critically acclaimed adaptation of Larry McMurtry's novel *The Last Picture Show*. And Burstyn was anxious to play the part. Blatty was impressed, and with Friedkin's newfound clout in Hollywood, the studio went with Burstyn. It was a part that would eventually win her another Oscar nomination and make her one of the most respected actresses in the business.

For the fulcrum role of Father Karras, the priest with grave doubts about his calling, a number of leading men were considered, including a young Al Pacino. But Friedkin wasn't impressed with any of them. Blatty and Friedkin went for a relative newcomer, Jason Miller, who had just won the Pulitzer Prize and Tony Award for his play *That Championship Season*. Miller was to achieve minor stardom and an Academy Award nomination for his work in *The Exorcist*. The part of the exorcist—Father Merrin—was handed to Max von Sydow, a veteran Ingmar Bergman leading man who had been introduced to American audiences in 1965 when he played Jesus in George Stevens's respectable failure *The Greatest Story Ever Told*. After that part, having von Sydow play a Catholic priest was practically typecasting.

Literally hundreds of young girls were seen and tested for the plum role of Regan, the possessed daughter, but it finally landed in the lap of twelve-year-old Linda Blair, who had previously done mostly commercial work. Linda Blair's performance was to win her a Golden Globe and an Oscar nomination, but the controversy later stirred up about who had actually played the part may have lost her the Oscar.

The filming of *The Exorcist* has been chronicled elsewhere, so it need only be mentioned here that the shooting was plagued with the kinds of problems only a devil could imagine. Sets burned down mysteriously. Death threats were received on a regular basis from occult members. The film was hell to film. One of the supporting performers, Jack MacGowran, a famous Irish stage actor, died rather abruptly after completing his performance—just as his character had in the film.

Upon viewing the rough cut, without special effects or the completed sound track, Friedkin and Blatty knew they had something wildly different from anything anyone had ever seen before.

Warner Bros. announced *The Exorcist* as their big Christmas film for 1973. Friedkin and Blatty worked a crew around the clock to reach their December 26 deadline. But another deadline loomed before them. In order to qualify for the technical awards of the academy, the film had to be screened for the technical branches before December 19. So on that Friday night, December 19, Friedkin showed a not-quite-finished print of *The Exorcist* to two full houses at the Academy Awards Theatre on Melrose Avenue. Fortunately, one of the authors of this book, Jeff Burkhart, attended the second screening that evening and, without advance warning, saw what was the most horrifying film he had ever seen in his life. The audience was bewitched, spellbound, and deliriously thrilled as the film unfolded in its often jolting fashion. The language coming out of the mouth of a twelve-year-old was outrageous. The special effects were awesome. The acting and direction were superb, and on an intensity level the film was emotionally draining. It took more than one tranquilizer to put many of those first-nighters to sleep that evening. Word spread quickly that *The Exorcist* was a knockout, the most graphic and realistic horror film ever made. By the time it opened on December 26 in limited engagements, it had lines running on for blocks, with virtually every performance sold out. There was no doubt about it—*The Exorcist* had come to the screen intact and was going to be one of the most financially successful films in movie history. The *Newsweek* cover celebrating the success of the film and the huge resurgence into the occult merely confirmed the expectations held by the studio for its film.

The depiction of Regan's demonic possession was particularly original and compelling. Everything about her was vile, especially her contortions and her gravelly, raspy baritone voice howling with satanic delight and unleashing a torrent of profanities unheard on any screen before. The fact that this was supposedly being done by a twelve-year-old girl shocked many, and protests against the film arose for this very reason. But soon another actress, Linda Blair's double, was taking credit for the more horrific moments, and then an Academy Award–winning actress emerged, claiming credit for the voice of the demon who possessed Regan.

Mercedes McCambridge was a Hollywood veteran who had won an Oscar as Best Supporting Actress in 1949 in Robert Rossen's screen version of Robert Penn Warren's prize-winning novel *All the King's Men*. McCambridge was later nominated for a supporting part in George Stevens's production of *Giant* (1956), but after that her screen appearances grew fewer and far between. She'd continued to work on television and the stage, so it wasn't particularly big news when Friedkin hired her to loop some of Linda Blair's dialogue. However, when the film was initially released, McCambridge received no billing, although she'd been promised it by the director, according to the actress. And when *The Exorcist* became a blockbuster, McCambridge alerted the media; soon after, Friedkin admitted using her as the voice of the demon, and subsequent copies of the film bore her credit in the end roll-up. As for the stunt double, Friedkin said she was on the screen for less than thirty seconds and could hardly take credit for Linda Blair's performance. Still, from that time forth, many people questioned just how much of the demonically possessed Regan was actually Linda Blair's performance.

The Exorcist received ten Academy Award nominations, including ones for Best Director, Best Screenplay, Linda Blair, Ellen Burstyn, Jason Miller, and Best Picture, the first time a horror movie was ever recognized as such by the academy. This infuriated many of the older members of the academy, including director George Cukor, who publicly blasted the film and threatened to quit the academy if the film won.

Cukor's statements were highly criticized, but they might have had an impact, for come Oscar night the only major award *The Exorcist* won was Best Screenplay. For Best Picture, *The Exorcist* lost to a second-rate crowd pleaser, *The Sting,* starring Paul Newman and Robert Redford.

Ellen Burstyn went on to win the Oscar the following year for her sharp performance in Martin Scorsese's *Alice Doesn't Live Here Anymore* and has remained active in films, television, and stage. Jason Miller never lived up to the promise he showed in *The Exorcist* or as a playwright. Linda Blair continued to make horror films, each one schlockier than the next. And William Friedkin, who was the town's hottest director, quickly slipped with a series of overindulgent films, never to repeat the success he had achieved with *The Exorcist*.

It took nearly twenty more years before the horror genre

would, at last, become respectable with Jonathan Demme's riveting production of *The Silence of the Lambs*. Demme's film swept the Oscars, winning Best Actor, Best Actress, Best Script, Best Director, and, finally, Best Picture of 1991. Once and forever, *The Silence of the Lambs* gave horror films a good name.

There has never been, nor will there ever be, anyone quite like Frank Sinatra. In a glorious career that has spanned well over fifty years, Sinatra has been called the greatest pop male vocalist of the twentieth century. He has enjoyed immense success as a concert performer all over the world, is an award-winning actor both on film and in television, and, most important, is a recording artist whose records and albums have consistently hit and stayed on the charts. He's known today in the entertainment world as the Chairman of the Board,'' but back in 1951, just a little over a decade after his skyrocketing debut, Frank Sinatra could not even get himself a job.

As a young crooner from New Jersey, in the early forties Sinatra caused ''bobby-soxer'' hysteria in his early concert performances from the stage of the Paramount Theatre in New York City. No one had ever been so publicly fawned over and adored. Women of every age screamed at his very appearance, and swooning became synonymous with Sinatra. The thin Italian crooner soon saw his recordings skyrocket on the hit parade. Insiders who at first dismissed Sinatra, later considered him heir apparent to the throne long held by Bing Crosby. And as Crosby had done before him, Sinatra branched out into films. Louis B. Mayer put him under contract at Metro-Goldwyn-Mayer and featured him in a series of hit musicals, usually costarring Gene Kelly. His first big splash came in 1945 in *Anchors Aweigh* and his success continued throughout the decade, most notably in *Take Me Out to the Ball Game* (1948) and in the screen version of Leonard Bernstein's *On the Town* (1949). Although the studio publicity department painted the private Sinatra as a good family man, a practicing Catholic, and a tireless worker for numerous charities, those in the know revealed him to be a tough guy with an egomaniacal capacity for women and alcohol. After his divorce from his first wife, Sinatra fell headfirst for the gorgeous Ava Gardner, whom many saw as his match.

Ava Gardner first became known in the early forties as the wife of Mickey Rooney, one of Metro-Goldwyn-Mayer's biggest stars. Her wonderfully sultry looks and up-front attitude made this Georgia peach ripe for stardom. After appearing in *The Hucksters* (1947) with Clark Gable, Gardner was loaned out to RKO for the film version of the Broadway musical by Kurt Weill *One Touch of Venus*. As the statue of Venus who suddenly comes to life when kissed by a window dresser, Gardner struck the public's fancy. In 1951 her performance in M-G-M's film version of the Broadway hit *Show Boat* made her one of the biggest stars in Hollywood. Off screen, Miss Gardner was known as a girl out to have a good time at any cost, drinking the best of them under the table.

When Gardner and Sinatra connected and were finally married, it was like two storms colliding into a hurricane. But it was Gardner who made the most of it, and by 1951 she was a bigger star than her husband. In fact, Sinatra's career at that point was at an all-time low. His films had become silly and passé. His vocal cords had become infected, and this strained his singing

Frank Sinatra's comeback performance not only resurrected his career but also won him an Oscar.

voice terribly. For once, his records were no longer selling. No one seemed to want Frank Sinatra unless it was to reach his wife, Ava Gardner. Many thought his career was over when he went to Africa with Gardner, who was starring with Clark Gable in John Ford's remake of Gable's 1932 classic *Red Dust,* this time around called *Mogambo.* Sinatra trailed after his wife like a little lost dog, and it looked as though he had a new career as ''Mrs. Ava Gardner''—until their temperaments eventually ended the marriage.

Around the time the recording industry was delighting postwar America with tunes made popular by Bing Crosby, Judy Garland, Frank Sinatra, and Doris Day, the publishing industry was electrifying its readership with a new kind of novel from original voices, focusing on the World War II experience. Critics lavished praise on the first novel by a very young Norman Mailer entitled *The Naked and the Dead,* while the 1948 Pulitzer Prize for fiction went to a newcomer named James A. Michener for his stirring *Tales of the South Pacific,* the basis for the smash hit Rodgers & Hammerstein musical *South Pacific.* Leon Uris became a number one best-selling author with his powerful *Battle Cry.*

But, unquestionably, *the* most popular and extraordinary novel of World War II to emerge was James Jones's eight hundred-page opus about army life in Honolulu just prior to and during Pearl Harbor, powerfully entitled *From Here to Eternity.* This brutal but nevertheless monumental story, which was highly critical of the prewar U.S. Army, became the most talked-about book of the postwar years. To many observers, the Jones epic was unfilmable since it tackled highly censorable topics for its day, including homosexuality. Thus many viewed with skepticism the purchase of the film rights to *From Here to Eternity* by Columbia Pictures' tyrannical president, Harry Cohn. And for a long time, as endless scripts by a fleet of screenwriters failed to capture the essence of the novel, it seemed these Cassandras would be proven right. Finally a young screenwriter named Daniel Taradash took an original and lean approach to the novel and wrote a superb treatment of the book.

Buddy Adler was given the job of producing *From Here to Eternity* for Harry Cohn. Adler suggested Fred Zinnemann to direct. Zinnemann was a well-respected new director who had been nominated for an Academy Award for his moving postwar drama *The Search* (1947). He had also directed Marlon Brando in his first film, *The Men* (1950), and had made the western modern with his minimalist approach to the genre in *High Noon* (1952). Harry Cohn didn't like Zinnemann, particularly after the film he had made for Columbia that year, a beautiful rendition of Carson McCullers's achingly exquisite coming-of-age play, *The Member of the Wedding,* failed at the box office. Still, *High Noon* had been such a substantial hit that Cohn gave in and hired Zinnemann to direct *From Here to Eternity.* Unfortunately, according to the director, their initial meeting to discuss casting was very tense.

The screenplay of *From Here to Eternity* revolves around an army lifer named Prewitt, a stocky loner who, after blinding someone in the ring, refuses to grant his commander's request to see him fight for the company. For his stubbornness, Prewitt is given "the treatment," a harsh, unfair, and punishing army existence. Meanwhile, the commander's wife is a loose woman who is having one of her many affairs with her husband's right-hand man. Prewitt becomes involved with a whore he meets in Honolulu, and these two stories finally collide on Pearl Harbor Day.

Cohn wanted one of his two contract players to star as Prewitt, either Aldo Ray or John Derek. Zinnemann was appalled; for him only one man could play the part—Method actor Montgomery Clift. Cohn hated Zinnemann's idea, but he knew it was right. Clift was thus chosen for a role he was eager to play.

For the part of the commander's right-hand man, Cohn suggested Edmond O'Brien, but Zinnemann and Buddy Adler opted for Burt Lancaster, this time going for type. Lancaster was a natural for the part, and his price didn't scare off Cohn. So Lancaster was also set for the film.

For the critical role of the commander's wife, Cohn wanted Joan Crawford, a movie star enjoying a second comeback. But

Zinnemann felt Crawford was all wrong for the part and was especially displeased to hear that she was already selecting a stylish array of costumes for this rather drab woman, before meeting or consulting with the film's director. He determined to find a replacement for her and thus reserved judgment when Deborah Kerr's agent pitched his very British, very proper young actress to play the part of an army slut. After testing Kerr and hearing her amazingly flat American accent, Zinnemann knew she would exude a never-before-seen sex appeal in the role. So, once again, he persuaded Cohn to drop Crawford and cast against type with Kerr.

The part of Maggio, Prewitt's only friend in the company who dies at the sadistic hands of the brig commander, was a sensational supporting role. Eli Wallach was Zinnemann's choice for the part, and Cohn agreed. Wallach had created a sensation on Broadway in Tennessee Williams's *The Rose Tattoo* and was currently in rehearsal for Williams's next opus, *Camino Real.*

Then, suddenly, Cohn became besieged with telegrams and telephone calls from Frank Sinatra, begging to play the part of Maggio. Sinatra recognized how valuable the part could be to his almost nonexistent career. But even more so, he knew Maggio inside and out. In his gut, Sinatra knew this guy, knew how to play him. But Cohn remained adamant: Wallach was to play Maggio. Sinatra's pleas went unanswered—until suddenly Wallach's agent upped his client's price and revised his availability as a result of his previous commitment to Elia Kazan and *Camino Real.* Cohn was outraged by this ploy and cabled Sinatra, who was then in Africa with his wife. If Sinatra paid his own way back to the States, Cohn said, Columbia would agree to a screen test.

Sinatra took the next plane back to Hollywood and tested for Zinnemann and Cohn. The results were impressive enough for Cohn to offer Sinatra the part of Maggio—for a paltry $8,000.

Sinatra snapped it up. Other sources have said that Cohn

gave Sinatra the part after the crooner's Mafia connections pressured the studio chief. (This story was popularized by Mario Puzo in his book *The Godfather,* where the movie mogul in question supposedly found the head of one of his prized horses under his satin sheets.) But Zinnemann denies this. He insists Sinatra's brilliant screen test and his acceptance of Cohn's insulting salary offer got him the part. In any event, Frank Sinatra was announced in the part, much to everyone's surprise and skepticism.

Donna Reed was under contract at Columbia, and although she had played only "nice girls" prior to this, she fit Jones's description of Lorene, the Honolulu prostitute. Thus, another role was cast against type.

From Here to Eternity began shooting in Honolulu. Montgomery Clift had come to the role of Prewitt totally prepared; he had even learned to box and play the trumpet. Ever the consummate actor, he generously took Sinatra under his wing, guiding him in his performance as much as Zinnemann did. The two actors developed a strong relationship during the filming, often getting drunk together. Clift also exerted an enormous influence over Donna Reed, who had the majority of her scenes with him. Zinnemann was pleased by this and excited by the unexpected depth of Reed's and Sinatra's performances. Meanwhile Kerr and Lancaster became a sexually dynamic duo. Their love scene on a deserted beach was to become one of the steamiest ever captured on film.

The film opened in August of 1953 and was a smash. The critics couldn't find enough praise to lavish on it. To accommodate the crowds, extra morning and midnight performances had to be set up, breaking box office records everywhere. Lancaster and Kerr were the hottest screen lovers of the moment, and Donna Reed astonished audiences with her performance. But the biggest news was the comeback of Frank Sinatra in the part of Maggio. Montgomery Clift had given the performance of his

Nice girl Donna Reed won an Oscar playing a prostitute in From Here to Eternity.

life and in doing so had grounded the film with tremendous power, but it was Sinatra as the weasely but lovable wop who stole the picture. His death scene showed a dramatic range he had never previously been able to explore. Once more, Sinatra was on his way to the top. Everyone loved *From Here to Eternity* except its creator, James Jones, who felt the film had ruinously watered down his novel.

From Here to Eternity won the New York Film Critics Awards for the Best Film, Best Director, and Best Actor (Burt Lancaster) of 1953. The following spring it was nominated for thirteen Academy Awards, including Best Picture, Best Actor (Lancaster and Clift), Best Actress (Kerr), Best Supporting Actress (Donna Reed), Best Director, Best Screenplay, and, of course, Best

Marlon Brando visited director Fred Zinneman and star Montgomery Clift on the set.

Supporting Actor—Frank Sinatra. Clift really felt he deserved to win, but the award was given to William Holden for his performance in *Stalag 17*. Donna Reed won Best Supporting Actress, and Zinnemann and screenwriter Daniel Taradash were honored as well. The film won a total of eight Oscars, including Best Picture. And Frank Sinatra made the biggest comeback of the year when he won for Best Supporting Actor as Maggio.

Almost everyone associated with the film benefited in some way. Burt Lancaster became a major movie star and would be nominated for three more Oscars, winning as Best Actor of 1960 for Richard Brooks's hearty version of Sinclair Lewis's *Elmer Gantry*. Miss Kerr became one of the biggest names in film during the fifties and sixties and holds the record for seven nominations as Best Actress without a single win. Fred Zinnemann would be honored with three more nominations and a win in 1966 for *A Man for All Seasons,* and Daniel Taradash served as president of the Academy of Motion Picture Arts and Sciences for a number of years. Donna Reed moved to television with the very popular "Donna Reed Show," which ran on

Burt Lancaster and Deborah Kerr made film history for this torrid love scene on the beach.

ABC for several years and is still in syndication. Montgomery Clift did not fare as well as the others. Two years after the film, he suffered facial damage as the result of a terrible car wreck and became dependent on drugs and alcohol. His career faltered, and though he continued to give rich performances and was even nominated for an Oscar for his role in *Judgment at Nuremberg* (1961), his personal life was a hellish, headlong course of self-destruction. He died in 1966 at the age of forty-six.

And Frank Sinatra? Well, he never looked back after *From Here to Eternity*. He was to be nominated two years later for Best Actor in Otto Preminger's groundbreaking film about drug addiction, *The Man with the Golden Arm*. His film career was revitalized for the next thirty years, and he once more became the most popular male vocalist in America. He even survived Elvis Presley, rock and roll, the Beatles, and Michael Jackson, not to mention a third marriage to a very young Mia Farrow. A street is named after him in Palm Springs, as are several college auditoriums. And he remains, to this very day, "the Chairman of the Board." But none of this would have happened if *From Here to Eternity* hadn't happened along to resurrect his career.

GONE WITH THE WIND (1939)

I t seems unusually fitting that the most famous American motion picture of all time would have had the most famous casting history as well. No other film had lavished upon it the kind of worldwide attention engineered by David O. Selznick and his associates. At a time when the world was on the brink of a cataclysmic war, that a mere casting search for an actress to play a role in a film could have constituted front-page material seems incredible. But such was the case with *Gone With the Wind*. And even more striking is that all the hoopla paid off brilliantly—the perfect Scarlett was found. In fact, much of Margaret Mitchell's Civil War epic is so extremely well cast, all the noise may have been worth it.

The history of *Gone With the Wind* began when a young southern woman fell ill and to pass the time began working on a novel, based on relatives who had been part of the Civil War and Reconstruction era in the Old South. The young woman incorporated much of what had been told to her by her grandfather. She continued writing her historical romance, now of epic proportion, over the following decade, never considering it for publication. But after its completion the woman's husband persuaded her to show the novel to a visiting editor from Macmillan and Company, a publishing firm in New York City. Reluctantly, she did so. The editor took the manuscript back with him on his train ride from Atlanta to New York, and by the time he had reached his destination he had decided to publish the lady's first novel, called *Gone With the Wind*. The author, a quick-witted journalist named Margaret Mitchell, never anticipated that upon its initial publication in June of 1936, her book would immediately become the most popular novel ever written in this country. By the end of the year *Gone With the Wind* had outsold every other book in the country, with the exception of the holy Bible. And her record stands to this very day. Moreover, *Gone With the Wind* repeated its spectacular success abroad, supporting reprints in dozens of languages. Everyone was talking about *Gone With the Wind* and Scarlett O'Hara, perhaps the most brilliant heroine depicted in the English language since *Vanity Fair*'s Becky Sharp a hundred years before. It was hardly a surprise to anyone when Miss Mitchell was awarded the Pulitzer Prize for fiction in 1936.

Of course news had spread quickly throughout the publishing world, prior to *Gone With the Wind*'s official publication date, that something extraordinary was on the horizon. The word sprinted just as quickly throughout Hollywood, which was always ready to swoop down on a "hot new property."

Among those interested was an ambitious young woman named Kay Brown, recently hired by David O. Selznick as East Coast story editor for Selznick-International, his newly created production company financed by millionaire Jock Whitney. Selznick, Brown knew, was always keen about transferring literary material to the screen; already he'd had great success with two of Charles Dickens's best-known novels, *David Copperfield* (1935) and *A Tale of Two Cities* (1936). Thus, after

Clark Gable as Rhett Butler and Leslie Howard as Ashley Wilkes, a role Mr. Howard loathed.

Brown read *Gone With the Wind* in galley form, she insisted Selznick read it while on a cruise to Hawaii with his wife. Upon Miss Brown's strong recommendation, Selznick optioned the film rights to *Gone With the Wind* for $50,000, a stunning price at that period for a first novel by an unknown writer. Miss Mitchell accepted the offer when her publishers at Macmillan insisted she'd never receive a higher offer. Besides, she had seen Selznick's *David Copperfield* and had loved it, so she felt her property was in good hands.

When *Gone With the Wind* mania broke right after the novel appeared in bookstores across the nation, Selznick suddenly realized the kind of public scrutiny his production would no doubt encounter. The multitude of memos he dispatched on that very subject over the next three years indicated the responsibility he felt toward delivering a screen version faithful to the novel and its millions of readers—a responsibility that dealt with "the public trust." Understandably, Selznick sought a way to turn the hoopla generated by the book's overwhelming popularity into free publicity for his film.

And thus began the biggest casting search in the history of films—the search for Scarlett O'Hara.

Publicist extraordinaire Russell Birdwell was the first to suggest to Selznick, showman extraordinaire, the notion of organizing a national search for *the* actress to interpret the role of Scarlet on screen and thus creating a public carnival of national importance. Selznick immediately began mapping out a strategy to fit the campaign.

First he hired his trusted old friend and colleague George Cukor to direct the film. Their early careers had often crossed paths, to their mutual pleasure. Under Selznick's reign as head of production at RKO in the early thirties, Cukor had come into prominence as a first-class film director with such hits as *A Bill of Divorcement* (1932) and *Little Women* (1933). It was also at this time that Cukor became a great intimate of Selznick's wife, Irene, daughter of Louis B. Mayer, all-powerful czar of Metro-Goldwyn-Mayer. When Selznick moved over to Metro-Goldwyn-Mayer to head up production under his father-in-law, Cukor came along. There he directed *Dinner at Eight* (1933) and *David Copperfield* (1935), two of the studio's best films under Selznick's banner. So it was hardly a great surprise when Selznick offered *Gone With the Wind* to Cukor in 1936. Besides, Cukor had already gained a superb reputation as a "woman's director," eliciting especially fine performances from many of Hollywood's leading actresses, including Jean Harlow, Katharine Hepburn, and Greta Garbo; since *Gone With the Wind* revolved around Scarlett O'Hara, who better to direct the film than Cukor?

Once Cukor had been brought on board, three men were dispatched by Selznick and Birdwell to begin the nationwide search for Scarlett. Charles Morris was to comb the West, Oscar Serlin was responsible for the North and the East, and Max Armon was given the South. George Cukor accompanied Armon around the South. This extensive ploy was to continue for nearly a year, and the end result produced neither Scarlett nor the book's second leading female character, Melanie Wilkes. In fact, the only discovery made was Alissa Rhett, who would eventually play Melanie Wilkes's sister-in-law, India Wilkes.

The Hollywood search for Scarlett began with two formidable stars, Katharine Hepburn and Bette Davis. In speaking with Cukor and Selznick, Hepburn made no secret of her interest in playing Scarlett. Cukor had directed Hepburn in her first film, *A Bill of Divorcement* (1932), for Selznick. Her performance was a breakthrough. Her next film, *Morning Glory* (1933), won her the first of four Academy Awards as Best Actress, but it was in Selznick's screen version of Louisa May Alcott's *Little Women* that Hepburn truly shone, demonstrating her versatility in the role of Jo. Under Cukor's direction Hepburn received her second Academy Award nomination for Best Actress. She then went on to make a number of other films, including *Alice Adams* (1935) for George Stevens and *Sylvia Scarlett* (1936) for Cukor, but by 1936 the public was beginning to lose some of its fascination for

Vivien Leigh as Scarlett O'Hara with Hattie McDaniel as Mammy. Both won Academy Awards for their performances.

the strong-willed New Englander. This naturally concerned Selznick, but in 1936 Hepburn was still a potent force. More to the point, Selznick felt Hepburn wasn't sexy enough to play Scarlett, and certainly not southern enough. He asked Cukor to ask Hepburn to make a test for the role, a somewhat insulting request considering the actress's status at the time. Hepburn refused to test, which worried both Selznick and Cukor. Still, Hepburn would remain a candidate until the very end of the search for Scarlett.

Bette Davis, at this time, was quickly becoming queen of the Warner Bros. lot. She had been wasted in films during the early thirties, and it was not until she played the hardened, whorish Mildred in *Of Human Bondage* (1934) opposite Leslie Howard that the studio and the public knew what to make of her. The following year, 1935, she had won the Academy Award as Best Actress for a rather inferior melodrama called *Dangerous*. Davis followed her Oscar triumph with a role in *The Petrified Forest* (1936), based on Robert E. Sherwood's hit play, but the film proved a better vehicle for her male costars, Leslie Howard and Humphrey Bogart. Afterward Davis was forced into starring in a barrage of clunkers for Warner Bros. She thus saw Scarlett as a role that could firmly establish her as a powerful actress in Hollywood. Her strong, vixenlike personality was well suited for the part. Casting Davis as Scarlett O'Hara was pretty "right on the nose," and no one knew this better than her boss, Jack L. Warner. He thus offered Selznick the following deal: He would lend out Davis for the film, but only as a package deal. His newest young star, Errol Flynn, would have to play Rhett Butler. This certainly interested Selznick, but Davis refused to play Scarlett opposite Flynn, whom she considered a handsome but inferior talent. By thus removing herself, Davis lost any chance of being in *Gone With the Wind*. Years later, in her autobiography, Miss Davis also laid the blame on director Cukor, who she felt wasn't too keen on her (Cukor always denied this accusation). Fortunately, Davis was able to exorcise her need to play a scandalous southern belle when she starred in William Wyler's southern melodrama *Jezebel* (1938). And much to Selznick's consternation, Miss Davis won her second Academy Award for *Jezebel* just as *Gone With the Wind* was beginning production.

As the search for Scarlett continued, another campaign began to secure the right actor to play the male lead in *Gone With the Wind*. Miss Mitchell's own description of the colorful and charming rogue Rhett Butler clearly pointed the way to the one and only man for the job—Clark Gable, the King of Hollywood. Everyone wanted Gable to play Rhett Butler, including Selznick. The only one who could not see Gable as Rhett Butler was Gable himself. He had already won an Oscar as Best Actor of 1934 for Frank Capra's screwball classic *It Happened One Night,* and he had received a second nomination as the dashing Fletcher Christian in Metro-Goldwyn-Mayer's award-winning adventure *Mutiny on the Bounty.* His macho image, terrific sense of humor, and good common sense had made him the number one favorite among moviegoers both male and female. He was on top of the heap, so why risk playing second fiddle in a film where he was clearly supporting the female lead? Thus, when offered the role, Gable turned it down and recommended Ronald Colman instead.

Ronald Colman was desperate to play Rhett Butler, thinking it "a ripping" idea. But his support in the Selznick-Cukor camp was short-lived. Gary Cooper was considered, but the public rejected the idea. In fact, over 90 percent of the polls taken and letters received by Selznick-International insisted upon Gable as Rhett.

Suddenly Selznick reckoned with the fact that he had to have Clark Gable or he would betray the public trust. Selznick went to his father-in-law, Louis B. Mayer, who had Gable under contract, to see if something might not be arranged. Then Selznick got very lucky indeed. Gable fell madly in love with one of the screen's most delicious actresses, Carole Lombard. Trouble was, Gable was already married to a woman seventeen years his senior, Rhea Langdom Gable. When Mrs. Gable learned of the affair, and her husband asked for a divorce, she demanded a fortune in settlement. Under his present contract at Metro, Gable could never hope to raise the $300,000 he needed to get rid of his wife and marry Lombard. But with a salary nearly four times his usual being offered by Selznick and a percentage of the film's business, he could pay off his wife and marry the fair Lombard.

So, finally, Gable accepted the part of Rhett Butler. And for his services, Mayer acquired the distribution rights to *Gone With the Wind* from David O. Selznick, a deal that eventually repaid Metro handsomely. For his part, Selznick would later on seriously miscalculate the film's future box office potential. In 1942, short on cash because of his extravagant gambling debts, he sold his interest in *Gone With the Wind* outright to Metro-Goldwyn-Mayer—forfeiting the millions of profit revenues the film would generate in its numerous studio rereleases. Today it is owned by Ted Turner and continues to excite audiences. *Gone With the Wind* is still *the* most popular movie ever made.

As the three casting directors searched all across the nation, looking for their Scarlett, Selznick and Cukor began interviewing and testing most of the established actresses in Hollywood, along with several unknowns submitted by agents. The screen tests alone would eventually cost nearly $100,000, an unheard-of sum at the time.

Jean Arthur had made a big noise in Frank Capra's *Mr. Deeds Goes to Town* (1936) and had a long-term relationship with Selznick, but her test wasn't very good. Miriam Hopkins was a wonderfully witty actress who had starred in Ernst Lubitsch's comedy classic *Trouble in Paradise* (1932) and had proven a delightful Becky Sharp in the 1935 film version of *Vanity Fair*. But although she was a very close friend of George Cukor, Hopkins had acquired a reputation for being mannered and difficult to work with. Loretta Young was discussed, but she refused to test, and nothing in her screen credentials made Cukor believe she could essay the role of Scarlett with all the aplomb needed. Kay Brown suggested an unknown British actress, then costarring with Laurence Olivier and May Robson in the costume drama *Fire over England* (1937). Selznick ran part of the film and was unimpressed by the dark-haired beauty he saw. He forged ahead, testing a young model with no screen experience whom his wife, Irene, had seen in a New York fashion show. Her name was Edythe Marriner, and her test wasn't especially good. But young Edythe persevered in Hollywood and eventually succeeded as Susan Hayward. The queen of the MGM lot, Norma Shearer, was considered, but when news reached the front page of the *New York Times,* via David Selznick, the public was outraged. To her credit, Miss Shearer wisely realized just how wrong she would be as Scarlett O'Hara. Broadway star Tallulah Bankhead, a southern aristocrat in her own strange way, made it known she'd like to play Scarlett, but she was offered the role of an Atlanta madame, Belle Watling, instead. Bankhead was insulted by the proposal and refused.

Two and a half years later Selznick was forced to start production on *Gone With the Wind* or else lose his financing and his star, Clark Gable. So in December of 1938, shooting began without a Scarlett. The list of real contenders had by this time dwindled. Joan Bennett was still in the running, but she lacked the authority the part demanded. A young unknown, Doris Jordan, was also on the short list; her test had proven very interesting. Frances Dee, however, was more an afterthought than a serious consideration. And, of course, there was still Katharine Hepburn; Selznick secretly confided to Cukor that if all else went wrong, he would use Hepburn. But the number one contender for Scarlett was, oddly enough, Selznick's next-door neighbor, Paulette Goddard, wife of comic genius Charlie Chaplin.

Paulette Goddard had made an impressive film debut opposite her husband as a gamine in his amazing 1936 classic *Modern Times*. Afterward her career seemed to stall, even though she was looked upon as a star with enormous promise. Her tests as Scarlett showed the necessary charm and vixenlike qualities. So, as 1938 drew to a close, Selznick and Cukor agreed to cast Goddard as Scarlett. A contract was negotiated—and then a bomb went off.

Goddard and Chaplin claimed to have been married aboard a ship in the Bay of Hong Kong, but neither one could come up with a marriage certificate. About this time the threat of communism was surfacing in Hollywood. A Red scare terrified the community, and the number one "Red" was thought to be Chaplin himself. The fact that Miss Goddard had possibly been living in sin, and with a Red, infuriated the country. Thousands of protest letters were received by Selznick-International, threatening a boycott of the film. Because these threats were taken seriously, Miss Goddard's chances of playing Scarlett grew ever thinner.

Thus, when filming of *Gone With the Wind* began with the burning of Atlanta, a stunt double was used for Scarlett. That production had actually started seemed like a minor miracle to producer and director, but a major miracle was about to happen on that very evening.

Vivien Leigh was, at that time, unknown in America. A singularly beautiful and intelligent actress, she had garnered good notices from the West End critics for her stage performances in London during the 1930s. While still married to an older man, Leigh had fallen desperately in love with England's brightest new talent, Laurence Olivier, who was still married to actress

Jill Esmond. The two of them appeared in *Hamlet* in what is re-called as a classic production. Next they appeared in an Elizabe-than costume epic for Alexander Korda—*Fire over England* (1937)—which Kay Brown had seen in New York. Based on this film, Brown recommended her to Selznick, who was unim-pressed by Leigh after seeing only part of the film. But Leigh had read *Gone With the Wind,* and she was determined to play Scar-lett. She knew the odds were against it, but apparently there was more of the willful Scarlett O'Hara in Miss Leigh's soul than anyone imagined.

In 1938 Laurence Olivier was offered the plum role of Heathcliff in Samuel Goldwyn's production of Emily Brontë's Gothic love story *Wuthering Heights.* William Wyler, set to di-rect the film, met with both Olivier and Miss Leigh in London. Wyler offered Leigh the role of Isabella in the film, but she sought the lead role of Cathy, which was already promised to Merle Oberon. Wyler insisted that no better a part would serve as Miss Leigh's introduction to Hollywood than that of Isabella. But Leigh didn't feel this was true and turned the role down. Olivier left for Hollywood and Leigh went into a play in Lon-don, but not before meeting and befriending Olivier's clever movie agent, Myron Selznick, the brother of David O.

The separation between the two lovers became intolerable, especially to Miss Leigh, who found herself with a lot of time on her hands when her play folded. She decided to come to Holly-wood to be with Olivier. She had also decided she would have a much better chance of playing Scarlett if she appeared in person. On the boat crossing the Atlantic and on the train carrying her to California United States, Leigh read and reread Mitchell's book, memorizing various passages and rehearsing herself in several of the scenes. By the time Leigh arrived in Los Angeles, she had become Scarlett O'Hara. Her fierce determination was immediately apparent to Myron Selznick, and he knew he had found the right Scarlett.

On the very night Atlanta was being burned down, Myron took his new client, Vivien Leigh, to meet his brother on the set. He introduced her to David as "his Scarlett." And after just a few moments with Miss Leigh, Selznick knew his brother might be right. A test was made immediately, and Leigh proved perfect. She suddenly became the dark horse contender. Cukor was very impressed by Leigh's performance, and on Christmas Day, at a dinner at Selznick's house, Cukor and the producer told Miss Leigh and Mr. Olivier that, secretly, she had the part.

The signing of Vivien Leigh, an Englishwoman and an un-known to boot, as Scarlett O'Hara made front pages around the world. Suddenly everyone wanted to know all there was to know about Vivien Leigh. As shooting began in January, Miss Leigh was once again separated from Olivier, who had left for New York to play opposite Ina Claire in S. N. Behrman's so-phisticated ditty *No Time for Comedy* on Broadway.

Casting the other roles in *Gone With the Wind* was certainly not as arduous as finding a Scarlett or as expensive as securing Gable as Rhett. Still, the public was concerned. For the part of Ashley Wilkes, the gentleman Scarlett is obsessively in love with throughout the story, Ray Milland and Lew Ayres were originally considered. Milland had been Irene Mayer Selznick's idea. Robert Young was brought up, then dropped. Cukor and Selznick both felt Melvyn Douglas tested for the part superbly but was wrong physically. Ronald Colman, who would have been ideal as Ashley, was never made a formal offer. Finally, Leslie Howard signed on. Howard was a major star of the stage in London and New York and had been in a number of terrific films, including *The Scarlet Pimpernel* (1935) and *Pygmalion* (1938), for which he was nominated by the academy for his per-formance as Henry Higgins. Mr. Howard personally hated the part of Ashley, seeing him as a weak sister, but he was keenly aware of the scope *Gone With the Wind* might have and how it could benefit his film career.

The second female lead in *Gone With the Wind* is Ashley's spiritually strong but physically weak wife, Melanie Wilkes. Selznick's first choice was Janet Gaynor. Miss Gaynor was the first actress ever to receive an Academy Award, offered for her work in F. W. Murnau's Expressionistic landmark, *Sunrise* (1927). She had received another Best Actress nomination when she starred as Vicki Lester in Selznick's great Hollywood soap opera *A Star Is Born* (1937), opposite Fredric March. But Gaynor turned down the role of Melanie. She turned down everything, in fact, and retired from films. Elizabeth Allan, who had played David Copperfield's mother for Selznick and Cukor, was next brought under consideration, as was Anne Shirley, who had just played Stella Dallas's daughter opposite Barbara Stanwyck. Andrea Leeds was also tested for Melanie. Miss Leeds had made a strong impression as the suicidal actress in *Stage Door* (1937). Finally, Joan Fontaine, one of Selznick's new contract actresses, was approached. Although Miss Fontaine did not test, Cukor made it clear he wanted her as Melanie; but Miss Fontaine simply didn't like the part. She did suggest, however, that her older sister might be interested. Miss Fontaine's sister, who was under contract to Jack Warner, was interested, and did test, and Olivia De Havilland was announced as Melanie Wilkes. Miss De Havilland had already been in a series of epic hits, including two starring Errol Flynn: *Captain Blood* (1935) and the lusty and quicksilver *Adventures of Robin Hood* (1938).

Billie Burke, widow of Flo Ziegfeld, was offered the role of Scarlett's aunt Pittypat Hamilton. Miss Burke, a celebrated actress who had been absolutely inspiring as the social-climbing wife in Cukor's *Dinner at Eight,* turned down Pittypat and instead became immortal playing Glinda the Good Witch in the Victor Fleming production of L. Frank Baum children's classic *The Wizard of Oz* (1939), opposite the legendary Judy Garland as Dorothy. Laura Hope Crews was set as Aunt Pittypat, and no one could have been better in the role. Lillian Gish, first lady of the silent screen, turned down the role of Scarlett's mother, and Barbara O'Neil was hired in her stead. Lionel Barrymore was sought to play Dr. Meade, but by this time Barrymore was confined to a wheelchair, so Harry Davenport was brought on board. The rest of the cast included Evelyn Keyes and Ann Rutherford as Scarlett's younger sisters, Thomas Mitchell as her father, Gerald O'Hara, Victory Jory, Butterfly McQueen, and Hattie McDaniel as Mammy. The supporting characters were all perfectly cast and gave vivid interpretations.

Two weeks into filming, *Gone With the Wind* was hit by disaster. Clark Gable felt uncomfortable with George Cukor; he believed the "woman's director" was favoring Leigh and not paying enough attention to him. The actor's insecurity led him to publicly question the ability of a homosexual director to do justice to a strong male character. He wanted his old buddy Victor Fleming brought aboard.

Selznick bent to Gable's demands, for several reasons. First, Gable was the biggest star in the world at the time. Second, Selznick felt that Cukor's pacing was slow and that the film looked too gloomy. Thus, three weeks into production he fired both Cukor and the cameraman. Vivien Leigh and Olivia De Havilland were dumbfounded. They begged Selznick to keep Cukor, but he would not be dissuaded. Victor Fleming was still working on *The Wizard of Oz* at Metro, but Louis B. Mayer replaced him with King Vidor (who shot only the Kansas sequences of *Oz*), and Fleming took over *Gone With the Wind*.

Fleming and Gable got along swimmingly, but the director was hard on Vivien Leigh. Yet even he recognized she was giving an extraordinary performance. In truth, both Miss Leigh and Miss De Havilland were seeing Cukor secretly at night, accepting his direction for the scene they'd be shooting the following day. This went on for the next ten weeks. Selznick was always on the set, making comments and suggestions while revising the script constantly. Finally the pressure became too much even for a thick-skinned brute like Fleming. He suffered a nervous breakdown and quit the film.

Selznick next brough in Sam Woods, who had just completed *Goodbye, Mr. Chips* (1939) with Robert Donat. After eight weeks Fleming returned, and finally, by the end of twenty-two weeks of shooting with no less than six different units working simultaneously—and on a budget twice its original size—Selznick had a completed film.

In August of 1939 Selznick and his wife, Irene, along with the film's editor and financier Jock Whitney, took a rough cut of *Gone With the Wind* to Riverside, California, where it was secretly previewed. It ran four hours with an intermission, and after that preview they knew they had perhaps the best film ever produced in Hollywood. Selznick also knew his *Gone With the Wind* was every bit as good as Mitchell's book.

When *Gone With the Wind* opened that December, it validated all the hype created by Selznick and his associates. The producer's big gamble had hit the jackpot. Everyone loved *Gone With the Wind*, and it became the most successful film ever made. Vivien Leigh scored a huge triumph as Scarlett, and Clark Gable matched her perfectly as Rhett. Victor Fleming received sole credit as the director, though Cukor's influence can be felt throughout. The physical production surpassed anything previously attempted in American filmmaking, thanks to William Cameron Menzies's superb production design. Max Steiner's "Tara's Theme" became an instant standard.

Oddly enough, the New York Film Critics passed over *Gone With the Wind*, giving their top prize that year to *Wuthering Heights*, which had made an international star out of Laurence Olivier. In fact, the only award bestowed upon *Gone With the Wind* by that august body was the Best Actress trophy, offered to Vivien Leigh. But the Academy of Motion Picture Arts and

Sciences made up for the oversight with ten nominations of their own, including one for Leigh, Gable, De Havilland, and Hattie McDaniel.

The 1940 Oscar ceremonies showered *Gone With the Wind* with eight awards, and a special Irving Thalberg award went to David O. Selznick for his integrity as a producer. Fleming won for Best Director, and the recently deceased Sidney Howard won for Best Screenplay Adaptation. Clark Gable lost out to Robert Donat's sterling Mr. Chips; De Havilland came up short as Hattie McDaniel became the first black performer to win an Oscar in her supporting role as Mammy. But, as everyone expected, Vivien Leigh won for Best Actress.

Vivien Leigh and Clark Gable never worked together again. Gable married Carole Lombard in 1939, and it was an idyllic, loving match; but, tragically, Lombard was killed a few years later in a plane crash while selling war bonds. Gable's career was interrupted by World War II, but upon his return to films he was as popular as he had been in the thirties and remained Hollywood's King until his death in 1960.

Vivien Leigh married Laurence Olivier, and they became the most celebrated married couple in the public eye for almost twenty years. Although she was better in films, Leigh preferred to perform on stage, and she and Olivier appeared together in many stage productions, touring around the world. Unfortunately, what many assumed was the actress's self-indulgent display of temperament proved to be much more serious: Vivien Leigh was a hopeless manic-depressive whose condition would worsen with the years. She suffered many nervous breakdowns, which made it increasingly more difficult for her to secure work. However, she did repeat her London stage performance as Blanche du Bois in Tennessee Williams's masterpiece *A Streetcar Named Desire* when Elia Kazan directed the film version in 1951. Playing her second southern belle, Miss Leigh gave a performance of harrowing beauty; in fact, many consider it to be among the two or three finest female performances ever captured on film. For *A Streetcar Named Desire,* Leigh won her second Academy Award as Best Actress. Her film career never really flourished after *Streetcar,* and she died in 1967 of tuberculosis.

David O. Selznick never again duplicated the kind of magic he had created with *Gone With the Wind,* although he spent the rest of his career trying to top it. He won a second Oscar in 1940 for his memorable production of Daphne du Maurier's suspense classic, *Rebecca,* which was Alfred Hitchcock's first American film. Selznick tried to outdo *Gone With the Wind* with a sexy lust-in-the-dust oater called *Duel in the Sun* (1946), starring his new wife, actress Jennifer Jones, and Gregory Peck, but the film paled badly in comparison. Selznick feared that when he died he would be remembered only as the man who had made *Gone With the Wind.* And as it happened, when he finally did die of a heart attack in 1965, no longer a real player in Hollywood, his obituary everywhere began with "David O. Selznick, producer of *Gone With the Wind,* died today of heart failure. . . ."

Still, if one is to be known for a single film, *Gone With the Wind* is the film it should be. As an epithet, even for David O. Selznick, it can't be beaten.

Marlon Brando may possibly be the greatest actor this country has produced in the twentieth century. His artistry, powerful physical presence, and interpretive genius appear to be beyond the scope of all who have preceded him and—it may even be argued—all those who have followed him. His acting style is based on the Method principle, first used by Stanislavsky in Russia and later taught and practiced by the Actors Studio of New York under the leadership of Lee Strasberg and Stella Adler. Drawing upon his own experience for inspiration, Brando, at his best, brought forth this "interior" style of acting to astonish and delight his audiences. The Method differed greatly from the type of acting taught in England (and exemplified by Sir Laurence Olivier), which sought external means to bring truth to a performance—observation, rather than introspection. Although the Method had been practiced upon the American stage since the thirties, it became popularized by Marlon Brando, whose performances on both the stage and in films revolutionized American acting.

Brando originally gained recognition as a young actor on Broadway, appearing in *I Remember Mama* (1944) and *Truckline Cafe* (1946). But it was his historic performance as Stanley Kowalski in Tennessee Williams's *A Streetcar Named Desire,* under Elia Kazan's inspired direction, that made him a superstar on stage. His combination of street smarts, brute force, and un-adulterated sexuality brought an interpretation to Stanley that has haunted every production of *A Streetcar Named Desire* since 1947. When Brando repeated his performance in the 1951 film version, he was, quite simply, the sexiest man ever seen in an American movie.

Brando followed *A Streetcar Named Desire* with four films that clearly demonstrated his enormous range as an actor. The first was as Mexican revolutionary Emiliano Zapata in *Viva Zapata!* (1952), scripted by John Steinbeck and directed by Elia Kazan. Brando received his second Oscar nomination for it. His next film was no less than Joseph L. Mankiewicz's M-G-M prestige production of *Julius Caesar* by William Shakespeare. As Mark Antony, Brando proved beyond a doubt that he was not just a mumbling Method actor, but a gifted classical artist as well.

Father and sons. From left to right, Al Pacino, Marlon Brando, James Caan, and John Cazale.

This performance bagged him his third Academy Award nomination.

Brando's next film was a complete about-face, a low-budget movie about bikers and delinquents aptly entitled *The Wild One*. As a nearly illiterate but ultimately sensitive biker (à la Hell's Angels), Brando gave a performance that became nothing less than the basis for an international teenage rage. Finally, in Sam Spiegel's Oscar-winning production of Budd Schulberg's *On the Waterfront*, Brando reached nothing less than poetic perfection as Terry Molloy, the punch-drunk ex-fighter working on the union-corrupted waterfronts of New York and New Jersey. The part was originally intended for Frank Sinatra after his amazing comeback in *From Here to Eternity*, but Sinatra was phased out when Brando became available. Once again, under Kazan's direction, Brando was sublime and heroic, as well as incredibly sexy. He was nominated for his fourth Oscar, and this time he won as Best Actor of 1954.

The rest of the decade saw Brando in a variety of improbable roles, including Napoleon in the ill-advised *Désirée* (1954) and Sky Masterson in the bloated film version of *Guys and Dolls* (1955). He enjoyed several commercial successes, such as *The Teahouse of the August Moon* (1956) and particularly *Sayonara* (1957), for which he was nominated a fifth time by the academy. Unfortunately, he ended the fifties with a flop, a western he had produced and directed called *One-Eyed Jacks*. Still, in the early sixties, no other actor was as respected or as admired as Marlon Brando.

And then it all came tumbling down. Brando decided against playing T. E. Lawrence for David Lean in *Lawrence of Arabia* and opted instead to play Fletcher Christian in M-G-M's costly and misfired remake of the classic 1935 sea adventure *Mutiny on the Bounty*. The production was cursed practically from the onset. Sir Carol Reed was set to direct but withdrew just prior to shooting. Lewis Milestone replaced Reed, much to Brando's displeasure. The company hit the rainy season while filming in Tahiti, which delayed the production for weeks. Stories began to circulate that Brando's temperamental behavior on top of the stalled production had already doubled the budget to a whopping $20 million, a gigantic sum in the early sixties.

When the film was released, people were puzzled by the result. Brando had decided to play Fletcher Christian against type, making him a late-eighteenth-century English fop who looks as if he'd wandered aboard the *Bounty* by mistake. The critics admonished him for being self-indulgent, almost silly. The film was a fiasco, and many held Brando directly accountable. After *Mutiny on the Bounty,* his career never recovered.

The sixties were nightmare years for Brando. Physically his appearance had altered alarmingly. His once muscular body turned first to flab and then to downright fat. Worse than that, many found his performances self-parodying and flat. He did not have one commercial success throughout the decade, and more than a few were ready to write him off entirely.

Mario Puzo's sole purpose in writing his third novel, a Mafia family saga entitled *The Godfather,* was to make some quick cash in order to keep his family alive and pay off a few of his long overdue gambling debts. Puzo's first two novels had received critical acclaim but had failed to earn for its author an income. *The Godfather* would be different, Puzo concluded desperately. While still a rough first draft, his new novel was discovered by the energetic and witty head of creative affairs for Paramount Pictures, Peter Bart. Bart worked for the studio's boy genius production head, Robert Evans. Bart convinced Evans to buy the rights to *The Godfather* prior to its publication for a mere $50,000 and to hire Puzo to write a first-draft screenplay. And in so doing, Evans pulled off one of the great coups of the decade. For upon its publication in 1970, *The Godfather* gunned its way to the top of the best-seller lists and stayed there for over a year. It became the biggest novel since *Gone With the Wind* and made Puzo a very rich man indeed. After completing a set of revisions on the screenplay of *The Godfather,* Puzo was virtually dismissed from the production by Evans, a move Puzo resents bitterly to this very day.

Anxious to capitalize on *The Godfather*'s extraordinary success, Robert Evans began preproduction in 1970. On the other hand, Paramount's corporate owners, Gulf & Western, were a bit leery of *The Godfather,* fearing it would prove to be a financial fiasco like the 1968 Mafia-themed Paramount release, *The Brotherhood.* But Evans was determined to get the show rolling, so he placated the brass by presenting a relatively moderate budget for the production. Next he hired Francis Ford Coppola, fresh from a successful rewrite of *Patton* (1970), to rework the Puzo version. A dozen directors were approached to take on *The Godfather,* including Arthur Penn, Fred Zinnemann, Constantin Costa-Gavras, Richard Brooks, and Sidney J. Furie, but all of them passed for varying reasons. Finally Evans offered Coppola the chance to direct the film, and encouraged by his close associate, George Lucas, Coppola said yes. Once Paramount approved his version of the screenplay, which retained the novel's originality in presenting the Mafia chief and his murderous family as noble and tragically flawed, casting began on the most talked-about film of the year.

Who was going to play the title role of Don Corleone, the all-powerful Godfather, who ruled one of the five families that made up the Italian Mafia in the United States? Hundreds of people were interviewed, photographed, and tested. Anthony Quinn was mentioned quite frequently in the beginning, as was Raf Vallone. Ernest Borgnine was contemplated, and Richard Conte, and Evans even thought of using Sophia Loren's husband, producer Carlo Ponti. But no one impressed Coppola or Evans. At last they decided that if they couldn't find someone who actually looked like the Godfather, they'd hire the best actor in the world, someone who could convincingly *become* the Godfather.

The field was quickly narrowed down to two actors. Robert Evans considered Sir Laurence Olivier, while Francis Ford Coppola favored Marlon Brando. Coppola contacted Puzo to see how he felt about Brando. Puzo was delighted, but the Paramount brass were not. They preferred Olivier and actually made him an offer. Unfortunately, Olivier was waging his own private war against cancer, so he had to pass. From that point on Coppola began pushing Brando fervently.

Robert Evans and Frank Yablans, head of Paramount at the time, both stood firm in their conviction not to hire Brando. They saw him as a temperamental washout with no box office draw. Besides, he was ten years too young for the role; how could he possibly pull it off?

As all the other candidates failed to materialize, Evans finally agreed to using Brando—on three conditions. First, Brando would receive no money up front if he was hired. Second, any overages in cost due to Brando's behavior were to be paid out of the actor's salary. Third, and most difficult of all, Brando would have to test for the part, something he had never done before. Under these circumstances, Coppola was certain he faced an impossible mission. Imagine his surprise when Brando agreed to all three conditions! Without any pressure from Coppola, the actor even allowed him to videotape a test at Brando's home. And, of course, the test was incredible. Suddenly, before Coppola's eyes, Brando transformed himself into Vito Corleone, the Godfather.

The announcement of Marlon Brando as the Godfather, under the direction of Francis Ford Coppola, caused barely a ripple throughout the industry. In fact, insiders were suspect of the whole situation, and expectations for the film were lowered accordingly.

With Brando in place, Coppola focused his attention on the other major parts. The role of Michael Corleone, the Godfather's youngest son, was absolutely central to the story. Everything revolved around Michael, and in many ways *The Godfather* is his coming-of-age story. First choice was Robert Redford, and an actual offer was made to Redford, who, intelligently, turned it down. Warren Beatty followed suit, as did Dustin Hoffman. Rod Steiger began to campaign for the part, but since he was nearly thirty years too old for the role, he wasn't taken seriously. Robert Evans was high on using Ryan O'Neal, fresh from *Love Story* (1970), or possibly even Jack Nicholson; but their tests weren't particularly good. Martin Sheen was considered, as was Dean Stockwell and Tony Lo Bianco. Finally, a young new Broadway actor, Al Pacino, was given a screen test. Pacino had one film under his belt, the lead in the harrowing junkie epic *Panic in Needle Park* (1971). Everyone knew Pacino was talented, but his test was a disaster. He kept messing up his lines and, in the Brando tradition, mumbled unintelligibly. No one was impressed with him. James Caan was tested for the part, but he only made Pacino look better in comparison. Finally Coppola decided in favor of Pacino, and after pacifying the Paramount brass, he was allowed to offer the actor the role. Thus far *The Godfather* had a has-been and a nobody as its two stars.

Once more James Caan was considered, this time for the part of the don's oldest son, the hot-blooded, well-endowed Sonny Corleone. Caan fit this role perfectly and won out over another unknown actor who had tested—Robert De Niro. For the part of Tom Hagen, Coppola chose Robert Duvall, who had starred in Coppola's *The Rain People* the year before.

The role of Michael's waspy girlfriend, Kay, was next on the list. Jill Clayburgh, at the time Al Pacino's live-in girlfriend, tested first, and Susan Blakely and Michele Phillips were also tested. Ali MacGraw, Bob Evans's wife, was mentioned, as were Cybill Shepherd, Karen Black, and Anne Archer. But Kay was finally offered to Diane Keaton, who had previously been in the original Broadway cast of the rock musical *Hair,* followed by a comic turn in Woody Allen's *Play It Again, Sam.* There was nothing to indicate that she could play a dramatic role, but Coppola gave her the part anyway. A bit of nepotism might have been in play when Coppola cast his own sister, actress Talia Shire, in the role of Connie, the Godfather's only daughter. Finally, jazz songstress Morgana King was set as Mrs. Corleone after Anne Bancroft and Alida Valli both turned down the role.

So, there it was, a cast made up of relative unknowns, under the guidance of a director with a dubious track record, on what many hoped would be the biggest film of the year. To say things looked promising would, at that point, have been optimistic in the extreme.

The film began production in March of 1971 on locations in and around New York City. Prior to the actual first day of shooting, however, producer Al Ruddy conferred with mobster Anthony Colombo and struck up the following bargain: If Colombo would not interfere with the production, the words *Mafia* and *Cosa Nostra* would not appear anywhere in the sound track. Once this was agreed to, the film began shooting. But the mood on the set was far from ideal.

Al Pacino admitted to feeling insecure, always sensing he was about to be replaced by another actor. Robert Evans had to fight the Paramount front office no less than five times to keep Coppola as director. Nobody was getting a sense of what the film actually looked like, and Coppola kept revising the script, employing the aid of screenwriter Robert Towne for some doctoring.

One thing was certainly evident: Francis Ford Coppola was emerging as an artist in full control of his medium, using this opportunity to the best of his ability. Another thing that was apparent was Brando's amazing performance as the Godfather: he looked, smelled, and talked like Don Corleone. Brando was back in form, doing some of his finest work since his *On the Waterfront* days.

Filming concluded in July of 1971 on location in Sicily. Paramount had insisted that Coppola edit the movie in Los Angeles instead of up in San Francisco. This way Robert Evans could have more control of the final product.

The film opened in March of 1972 and ran three hours without an intermission. Nobody was really prepared for what Coppola had created in translating the novel to the screen; in many ways he had improved on the book while remaining utterly faithful to it. The film epic had a richness and scope that bordered on the operatic. Gordon Willis had photographed this dark tale in deep red shadows, and Nino Rota had written a haunting score. But the biggest news was Marlon Brando's performance as Don Corleone. Although the part was relatively small, Brando dominated the film from beginning to end. This was, without question, Brando's greatest triumph. And suddenly Brando was once again the biggest male star in the world.

Brando wasn't the only cast member to emerge triumphant from *The Godfather,* however. Al Pacino was a revelation as Michael, and many thought he walked off with the film. James Caan's portrayal of Sonny won him national recognition. Robert Duvall was given rave reviews from critics across the country. And Diane Keaton was recognized as a dramatic actress with style and wit. Everyone in the cast was magnificent.

The Godfather broke all previously existing box office records and repeated its success upon its worldwide release later that year. And the following spring the film received ten Academy Award nominations, including one to Brando as Best Actor and three in the Best Supporting Actor category—Al Pacino, James Caan, and Robert Duvall. Coppola was picked as one of the five Best Director candidates. The following month he won the Directors Guild Award for *The Godfather,* making him a sure thing for the Oscar.

But come Oscar night, *The Godfather* was nearly shut out by the striking John Kander and Fred Ebb musical *Cabaret. Cabaret* collected no less than eight Oscars, including one to Bob Fosse as the Best Director. Finally, *The Godfather* won Best Adapted Screenplay (Coppola and Puzo) and, next, Best Actor to Marlon Brando. But he sent an emissary to attend the ceremony in his place, so when it came time for Brando to pick up his award, one Sacheen Littlefeather appeared at the podium, saying that Mr. Brando was refusing the award because of the injustices the Indian nation were forced to endure. In the midst of this surprising turn of events, the ceremonies concluded with the final award—Best Picture of 1972—which went to *The Godfather,* netting the film a total of three Academy Awards.

The following year Brando stunned audiences with what many feel is his best performance to date, in Bernardo Bertolucci's *Last Tango in Paris.* As Paul, the grieving American in Paris who becomes sexually involved with a young girl in order to get past the pain in his own life, Brando was astonishing. For *Last Tango* the actor received his seventh Oscar nomination, but he lost to Jack Lemmon in *Save the Tiger.*

Meanwhile, most of the company, cast, and crew, of the original *Godfather* reunited to make *Godfather, Part II,* which was released at the end of 1974. It was, in many ways, vastly superior to the original and went on to win six Academy Awards, including Best Picture, Best Director, Best Screenplay, and Best Supporting Actor (to Robert De Niro as the young Don Corleone). The only actor missing from the film was Brando, but even so, his power could be felt throughout.

The two *Godfather* films came to be considered perhaps the

Robert De Niro achieved stardom and an Oscar as the young Don Corleone in
The Godfather, Part II.

finest American films of the 1970s and most assuredly the best
treatises ever on the influence of organized crime over American business and politics. In truth, *The Godfather, Part II* had not
been as successful financially as *The Godfather,* but the sequel was
seen as a work of art, the studio's great prestige achievement.
Therefore plans for a third installment were in the works.

During the early 1980s, Paramount trumpeted plans for *The
Godfather, Part III* starring John Travolta, still a potent box office
name at the time. Mario Puzo was fashioning an original screenplay while Coppola waited in the wings, reticent to commit.
Nothing ever materialized, however, and eventually *The Godfather, Part III* was left to simmer on a back burner.

Finally, nearly fifteen years after the release of *The Godfather,*
Paramount Pictures announced a major coup: Francis Ford
Coppola was to produce, direct, and cowrite *The Godfather, Part*

III, which would take up twenty years after *The Godfather, Part II.* This film would concentrate on organized crime's invasion on the international level, involving not only foreign governments, but the Vatican as well. Al Pacino would once again play Michael Corleone, Diane Keaton would be Kay, and Talia Shire would reprieve her role as Connie. Robert Duvall was approached to return as Tom Hagen, but his asking price of over $5 million ended any further discussion, and the character was written out of the film. The rest of the cast included such veteran character actors as Eli Wallach, George Hamilton, and Raf Vallone. Newcomer Bridget Fonda, Peter's daughter, Henry's granddaughter, and Jane's niece, was set for a flashy role as a news reporter.

In this part of the saga, Michael Corleone wants to go legitimate and hand over his reins as Godfather to his son, Anthony. But Anthony wants nothing to do with the family business and wishes instead to pursue a career as an opera singer. So Vincent Corleone, the illegitimate son of Sonny, is taken under Michael's wing as heir apparent. During this time, Vincent becomes emotionally involved with Mary Corleone, Michael's young daughter and Vincent's first cousin. Their love affair becomes the pivotal dramatic focus of the story, so proper casting of these two parts was critical to the film.

The first actor Coppola spoke to about playing Vincent was Robert De Niro, who had played the young Don Corleone in *The Godfather, Part II.* Unfortunately De Niro had a previous commitment, *Awakenings* which would have meant pushing back the start date on *The Godfather, Part III.* This Paramount would not hear of. The next serious contender for the part was Alec Baldwin, who would later score a Broadway triumph as Stanley Kowalski in the 1992 revival of *A Streetcar Named Desire* opposite Jessica Lange. Coppola continued to see other young actors as well, including Matt Dillon, Charlie Sheen, his nephew Nicholas Cage, Vincent Spano, and Kevin Anderson. Finally the director picked Andy Garcia, who had made an impression in a number of films, including *The Untouchables* (1987) and *Stand and Deliver* (1988), and was clearly the hottest new Hispanic actor on the scene at the time. As it happened, Garcia resembled Al Pacino not only in appearance, but in attitude as well.

Julia Roberts was Coppola's and Paramount's first choice as Mary, Michael and Kay's daughter, but Roberts was both unavailable and indifferent to the material. Such was not the case with "the material girl" herself, Madonna, who campaigned for the part and even met with Coppola at his ranch in Napa Valley,

Diane Keaton played Kay, Al Pacino's wife, in all three Godfather films.

California. For quite a while Madonna was a serious contender, but in the end Coppola decided she was simply too old to play Mary and continued his search. Ultimately he cast Winona Ryder in the part. Everyone greeted this news with enthusiasm, since Ryder was riding very high in the industry through her work in *Heathers* (1989), *Mermaids* (1990), and *Edward Scissorhands* (1990), costarring her then boyfriend, Johnny Depp.

Production of the $46 million film—seven and a half times more than the cost of the original *Godfather*—commenced in November of 1989 in Italy. Coppola had promised a final cut the following Christmas and faced stiff penalties if he did not meet this date. Thus, everyone was under terrific pressure.

One month into production Winona Ryder arrived in Rome to begin filming, having just completed *Mermaids* for Orion Pictures. The actress was physically and emotionally exhausted and showed it. Depp suggested she return to Los Angeles, so after several days, and under a doctor's recommendation, Ryder withdrew from the film.

Panic set in. The movie was already way overbudget and could not afford a costly delay. Coppola hurriedly considered Laura San Giacomo, who had made a name for herself in the low-budget hit *sex, lies, and videotapes* (1989), but then cast (to outcries of nepotism) his own daughter, Sofia—an inexperienced actress lacking the kind of sensual beauty the character required. Paramount and the rest of the cast and crew were shocked, but Coppola had the studio backed against a wall. Given the pressure of a stalled production, Paramount gave in and signed Sofia Coppola.

The Godfather, Part III experienced a multitude of problems, mainly budgetary. By the time the film wrapped, it had cost nearly $75 million. Still, the studio felt it was worth it. *The Godfather, Part III* was without question the most eagerly awaited film of 1990. Tickets for the first press screenings held in early December in New York and Los Angeles were prized possessions. All three major news networks covered the press screening as a major media event. Everyone wanted to know if Coppola had done it again. Was *The Godfather, Part III* a worthy sequel to the two previous films?

The answer from the first emerging audience was "No." No one wanted to negate all of the time and effort expended, but this costly production simply wasn't in the same vein as its predecessors. The plot was too baroque and much too confusing. The cast was generally praised, and Andy Garcia made quite a favorable impression as young Vincent. Immediately Oscar talk began to generate around him.

This was not the case with Sofia Coppola, who was almost universally felt to be the ruin of *The Godfather, Part III*. She was, at best, an immature actress who was way off base. Her awkward appearance and whiny, tinny voice had brought a $75 million production to its knees.

The Godfather, Part III was nominated for Best Picture that year, along with six other nominations, including one for Coppola and another for Garcia; but the film came out the evening's biggest loser. Financially, it never recouped its enormous budget, although it wasn't a total failure at the box office. Audiences initially went in droves but soon lost interest—not the best way to conclude the trilogy.

Coppola worked with Winona Ryder in his next film, *Bram Stoker's Dracula* (1992), and the results were pyrotechnical. Andy Garcia has made a number of films since but has yet to fulfill the promise shown in *The Godfather, Part III*. And Sofia Coppola hasn't made any other films of any note since her debut.

THE WIZARD

OF OZ (1939)

As far as movie moguls Louis B. Mayer, Darryl F. Zanuck, Jack Warner, and Adolph Zukor were concerned, the greatest casting coup of 1937 was not Garbo in *Camille* or Paul Muni in *The Life of Emile Zola* or Fredric March and Janet Gaynor in *A Star Is Born*. The greatest casting coup belonged to Walt Disney.

For the past three years Disney had been in production on the studio's first full-length feature, which insiders had dubbed "Walt's folly." When it was released in late 1937, *Snow White and the Seven Dwarfs* awed critics and overwhelmed the public, making it the box office champion of the 1937–1938 moviegoing season. And the coup was that Disney hadn't had to hire one live actor to actually appear on screen. Nobody had to worry whether Ms. White liked or disliked a costume or a piece of dialogue. The dwarves never flubbed their lines. No retakes were necessary. The cast was always at the studio, day and night, without a single complaint. Disney never had to deal with an actor or actress or a pestering agent. To the big boys, this was a dream come true—a smash hit with a make-believe cast.

What every major Hollywood studio took notice of was the mother lode of box office revenues a family fantasy feature could produce if it delivered the way *Snow White and the Seven Dwarfs* had. Not least among the animated film's many achievements was its amazing musical score. "Heigh-Ho," "Whistle While You Work," and the lovely "Someday My Prince Will Come" all became hit songs. So in January of 1938, while *Snow White* was enjoying a phenomenally successful wide release across the nation, Louis B. Mayer told his close buddy Arthur Freed to begin negotiating for the rights to L. Frank Baum's children's classic, *The Wizard of Oz* after Freed said he could make a terrific musical out of the material.

Arthur Freed was a Tin Pan Alley tunesmith who had cowritten with Nacio Herb Brown a catalog of songs that Mayer had used successfully in his Academy Award–winning 1929 musical, *Broadway Melody*. The score included "The Wedding of the Painted Dolls" and, most memorably, "Singin' in the Rain." Mayer liked the rambunctious Freed, a born self-promoter who was interested in producing for the studio but had been hired to head up M-G-M's musical department. Freed would use this position as leverage to maneuver his way into producing, but in 1938 his most valuable asset was his close friendship with Mayer. And although it's probably true that *The Wizard of Oz* began as his idea, Mayer knew he was too inexperienced to produce an expensive "prestige" film like *The Wizard of Oz*. Mervyn LeRoy was hired instead, with the understanding that Freed ride along as associate producer. Mervyn LeRoy agreed to these terms, and from that point on until his death in 1976, he insisted Mayer had purchased the rights to *The Wizard of Oz* with him in mind and not Freed. This point of contention was to last as long as both men lived.

Mervyn LeRoy was a director of note, responsible for a number of hits at Warner Bros., including *I Am a Fugitive from a Chain Gang* (1932) and *Anthony Adverse* (1936). Mayer brought him

W. C. Fields was the first choice for the Wizard, but he backed out over a salary dispute.

over to M-G-M in 1937, paying him a record $6,000 a week to make two films a year. LeRoy was as cocky as Freed, and the two had been friendly since 1923. Moreover LeRoy recognized Freed's musical expertise and welcomed the latter to his *Wizard of Oz* producing unit. But LeRoy bitterly resented Freed's constant reference to *The Wizard of Oz* as "his" picture. The fact that LeRoy had little experience with movie musicals, and that Freed would eventually become famous for his work in that genre, leads one to believe it was Freed who'd originally suggested *The Wizard of Oz* as the basis for a musical, but both men took credit for the notion.

When Louis B. Mayer sanctioned Freed to secure the rights to *The Wizard of Oz,* he wasn't the only one in town with the idea. In fact, he was one of five bidding up the purchase price from Sam Goldwyn who had bought the rights six years earlier for $40,000. At the time, 20th Century–Fox was very much in the bidding war, seeing it as the perfect vehicle for their number one box office star, Shirley Temple. But Mayer's $75,000 bid shut down the competition, leaving Goldwyn delighted to have made nearly twice his investment without ever shooting one reel on a family fantasy he was certain was unfilmable.

The first writer assigned to *The Wizard of Oz* was an odd choice, Herman J. Mankiewicz. Mankiewicz had written a brilliant screenplay adaptation of *Dinner at Eight* (1932), and his brother, Joe, had become one of M-G-M's finest young producers. But Herman had a volatile reputation as a gambler, a drunk, and a wit so cynical he could burst a string of rosary beads with a mere glance. Still, it was his idea to set the Kansas section of the film in black and white and the Oz portion in color. He was eventually dismissed and followed by no less than nine other writers, including Ogden Nash and Samuel Hoffenstein. But final credit went to Noel Langley, Florence Ryerson, and Edgar Allan Woolf, with Langley receiving sole adaptation credit. Most of these drafts were written under the authority of Richard Thorpe, the original director who was to quit the production before shooting commenced. Of course, LeRoy credited himself as supervisor for all the drafts, and, like clockwork, so did Arthur Freed.

Metro-Goldwyn-Mayer had, at that time, the largest roster of contract stars in the world. But Louis B. Mayer wasn't interested in anyone already working for the studio for the central role of Dorothy in *The Wizard of Oz.* He wanted one star and one star only, and he was willing to loan out Clark Gable and Greta Garbo in return for this star's services. She was only ten years old, and her name was Shirley Temple, and Miss Temple was

Shirley Temple was Louis B. Mayer's first choice for Dorothy, but 20th Century-Fox decided against it.

very much under contract at 20th Century–Fox.

It's probably a safe bet to say Shirley Temple was the biggest child star in movie history. She was number one at the box office for three years in a row (1935, 1936, and 1937), and her winning tap dancing, perky singing voice, and double-dimpled personality sent movie audiences through the roof. So it was perfectly natural for Mayer to want her as box office insurance for his costly fantasy film. But Fox, still smarting from having lost *Oz* to Mayer, told M-G-M to keep Gable and Garbo. They weren't giving up their Temple to anyone.

With Temple unattainable, Mayer, Freed, and LeRoy turned to M-G-M's stable and selected a sixteen-year-old singing star named Frances Gumm, aka Judy Garland. It was perhaps the best second-choice decision in American film history.

Judy Garland represented the very best and the very worst of the studio star system. The little girl with the extraordinary singing voice was put under contract to M-G-M in 1935, but physically Garland was not movie star material. She had a wonderful smile and an infectious laugh, but she was also a bit overweight, without doubt the "girl next door" type. Nevertheless, Mayer subjected her to the studio's grueling "glamour star" regimen—singing lessons, posture and poise classes, and acting coaching—all under the tyrannical supervision of her stage mother, Ethel Gumm.

Garland soon began to win public favor. In 1938, her version of "You Made Me Love You," sung to a photograph of Clark Gable, was a number one hit across the nation. And her performance as Betsy Brown in M-G-M's incredibly popular Andy Hardy family programmers gave Garland the kind of national exposure she needed. By the time she was cast as Dorothy, the studio had already spent five years developing her. Now they wanted to see if their investment would pay off.

Broadway dancing star Ray Bolger was a natural candidate for one of the singing, dancing supporting roles in *Oz*. Bolger had made a sensation in the 1936 Rodgers & Hart musical *On Your Toes*, where he'd miraculously danced the lead role in the famous George Ballanchine ballet "Slaughter on Tenth Avenue." He had also appeared as himself, his wiry long legs impressing movie audiences across the country, in M-G-M's Academy Award–winning film *The Great Ziegfeld* (1936). Bolger thought he was the ideal choice for the brainless but ever-so-wise Scarecrow, but Freed and LeRoy signed him on as the Tin Man. The role of the Scarecrow was given to song-and-dance man Buddy Ebsen, Shirley Temple's dancing partner in *Captain January*. Both men admired each other enormously, but all through rehearsals and costume fittings Bolger kept campaigning to switch roles with Ebsen. Finally his badgering wore everyone down, and just prior to filming the two actors did just that.

For the part of the Wizard of Oz, only one character actor was ideal for the role, as far as LeRoy and Freed were concerned—W. C. Fields. Fields had stolen *David Copperfield* (1935) as the bumbling, good-hearted Mr. Micawber, and everyone believed he would do the same as the Wizard. Thus,

The immortal foursome of Oz. From left to right, Jack Haley, Ray Bolger, Judy Garland, and Bert Lahr.

negotiations started. M-G-M offered Fields $75,000, but Fields demanded $100,000. Shocked at Fields's greedy counteroffer, Mayer refused. A disheartened LeRoy next offered the part to Ed Wynn, but the great vaudevillian had a very successful radio career and didn't feel the part was important enough to justify the time away from his broadcast obligations. Finally, contract player Frank Morgan was cast, and although Morgan lacked the instant recognizability of Fields and Wynn, he proved to be a delightful conman Wizard in his own right.

Only one person was ever considered for the Cowardly Lion—the great Broadway comic Bert Lahr. Lahr accepted the part and became part of movie folklore.

While Fanny Brice was under consideration as Glinda the Good Witch, the studio discussed the possibility of hiring the ever-popular character actress Edna May Oliver as the Wicked Witch of the West. But LeRoy felt Oliver was too ugly for the part; he saw the Wicked Witch of the West as a kind of seductive glamour puss and pushed for Gale Sondergaard, whom he had directed in *Anthony Adverse* (1936) to win the first Best Supporting Actress award ever. Miss Sondergaard expressed interest in the part, and a test was made. Miss Sondergaard's Wicked Witch—a kind of fallen hussy with green eye shadow and a sequined witch's hat—dismayed everyone but LeRoy and Sondergaard. Once again it was suggested that the Wicked Witch of the West be played as an ugly crone, but Miss Sondergaard refused to go along with the interpretation. In the meantime, Edna May Oliver had accepted a part in John Ford's *Drums Along the Mohawk* and was no longer available. So a relatively little-known B-contract player, Margaret Hamilton, accepted the part, one she had already played in a Junior League production in Cleveland. At the time, Miss Hamilton was thirty-six, just divorced, and supporting her three-year-old son. When she signed on for *The Wizard of Oz* it was for six weeks only, but by the time the film wrapped production, Miss Hamilton had been shooting for over four months.

Originally Fanny Brice was considered for Glinda the Good Witch, along with Constance Collier, Una Merkel, Cora Witherspoon, and even Edna May Oliver! But there was no contest when Billie Burke let it be known she was interested. Miss Burke, widow of the legendary Broadway impresario Florenz Ziegfeld, was a Broadway stage favorite and had proven extraordinary as the social-climbing wife in *Dinner at Eight* (1933) for M-G-M. Everyone was thrilled by the idea, and Miss Burke was cast immediately.

For the all-important job of composing the songs for *The Wizard of Oz,* Arthur Freed signed on the team of Harold Arlen and E. Y. Harburg. They proved to be an inspirational choice, composing one of the finest and most beloved original song scores ever created for a Hollywood musical. The studio's leading conductor, Herbert Stothart, was the musical adapter.

Filming began in Culver City in October of 1938 under Richard Thorpe's direction. Over a hundred midgets—the largest ever assembled in one place—had been secured to play the Munchkins. The cast was complete and ready to go, but within three weeks disaster struck—not once, but twice.

First, Buddy Ebsen was hospitalized after nearly dying from the aluminum spray makeup he was required to wear as the Tin Man. Ebsen was so allergic to the makeup that he remained in serious condition for several days. At last, because the front office insisted the production continue on schedule, Jack Haley was brought in as a replacement. Haley, a song-and-dance man of lesser fame, was to use the same costume, but a mask and different makeup were employed to avoid what had happened to Ebsen.

The second unexpected occurrence was the firing of director Richard Thorpe. Thorpe, who had directed such hits as *Night*

Must Fall (1937) and *The Adventures of Huckleberry Finn* (1939), was sustaining too slow and deliberate a pace on *Oz*. He seemed to lack a touch for fantasy, and the rushes reflected this. Victor Fleming, one of the studio's most reliable contract directors, stepped in to take his place.

Fleming was known as a "man's director" in much the same, unfair way George Cukor was known as a "woman's director." He had achieved some of the studio's biggest successes, including *Red Dust* (1932), *Treasure Island* (1934), *Captains Courageous* (1937), which had won an Academy Award for Spencer Tracy as Best Actor, and the rowdy *Test Pilot* (1938), starring Fleming's best friend and the studio's leading male star, Clark Gable. Fleming's work lacked the strong personal stamp so obvious in the films of Hitchcock or Lubitsch, but he epitomized everything Metro-Goldwyn-Mayer productions exemplified in the thirties—superb craftsmanship and the ability to stage a big story fluidly. He was also very good with actors and actresses, and for a "man's director," he managed to elicit quite a number of great female performances, including those of Jean Harlow in *Red Dust,* Judy Garland in *The Wizard of Oz,* Vivien Leigh in *Gone With the Wind,* and Ingrid Bergman in *Dr. Jekyll and Mr. Hyde* and *Joan of Arc.* So, after a brief interlude in which George Cukor took over the film for a few days, shooting recommenced with Victor Fleming in command.

The four months it took to film *The Wizard of Oz* were difficult and arduous. Fleming proved to be a tough taskmaster, although he was gentle with Garland and managed to bring out a fully developed performance way beyond anyone's expectations. Tempers were tested and temperaments strained all along the way, although everyone later said they loved making the film. Then, in its final three weeks, with only the black-and-white Kansas sequences left to be filmed, Victor Fleming was replaced as director.

George Cukor, it turned out, had just been fired from *Gone*

With the Wind after two weeks of shooting, and at Clark Gable's insistence David O. Selznick called in Victor Fleming as replacement. Because Fleming had not yet finished with *The Wizard of Oz,* King Vidor (who had directed Metro-Goldwyn-Mayer's first critical and commercial hit, *The Big Parade* in 1925) was brought in. Vidor filmed all of the black-and-white sequences, including Garland's poetic rendition of "Over the Rainbow." It is a credit to Mervyn LeRoy as producer that *The Wizard of Oz* appears to be so seamlessly directed.

The *Wizard of Oz* was one of the costliest productions ever made at Metro-Goldwyn-Mayer. Weeks before its scheduled opening in August of 1939, a preview was held in Santa Barbara. The audience felt that the film was special but too long, so one dance number was subsequently cut; but the producers, afraid the Kansas sequence was too sluggish, suggested "Somewhere Over the Rainbow" be cut as well. Harold Arlen, Yip Harburg, and Arthur Freed went to the wall on this—insisting it would be criminal to cut the song—and after a battle with Louis B. Mayer, they managed to save the piece.

When the film opened in August, it was greeted with mixed reviews. Some of the critics were absolutely enchanted by it, finding the sets, costumes, and songs a delight. But other critics complained, and one called it "downright dreadful." Yet initial audiences in the major cities across the nation were overwhelmingly positive. Box office business was more than brisk, Judy Garland was hailed as the brightest new star in Hollywood, and "Over the Rainbow" quickly began to climb the charts. But when the film began its second-run engagements, business slipped noticeably. Within months of its first release, *The Wizard of Oz* was running in the red, and it would take several reissues for it to make a theatrical profit.

The Wizard of Oz was nominated for Best Picture of 1939, along with *Wuthering Heights, Stagecoach, Ninotchka, Mr. Smith Goes to Washington, Love Affair, Goodbye, Mr. Chips, Dark Victory,* and *Of Mice and Men.* Oh, and the other Victor Fleming–directed picture of that year, *Gone With the Wind.* *Oz* was also nominated for its photography, sets, score, songs, and special effects. On Oscar night it lost out in most categories to *Gone With the Wind,* but it did manage to beat the Civil War epic for the Best Score, and Best Song was "Over the Rainbow." Judy Garland was honored with a special Oscar for her outstanding performances as a screen juvenile for the year.

The Wizard of Oz managed to recoup its investment only after a series of reissues during the 1940s and early 1950s. By then it had secured a place as a children's classic of the highest order. In 1955 *The Wizard of Oz* was televised to enormous ratings and has been shown every year since as an annual television event. It is one of the largest videocassette sellers of all time and continues to be reissued in theaters across the country.

Judy Garland's career skyrocketed with her touching performance as Dorothy, which is as endearing today as it was over fifty years ago. Indeed, "Over the Rainbow" would remain Garland's signature song for the rest of her life. Miss Garland quickly became one of the studio's biggest musical commodities. She appeared in a number of successful juvenile musicals costarring Mickey Rooney before coming beautifully to maturity in the glorious *Meet Me in St. Louis* in 1944. M-G-M's investment in plump little Frances Gumm had paid off in spades.

But with all that fame came tragedy as well. Garland was living on borrowed time, hooked on drugs and becoming increasingly difficult to work with. After two failed marriages she attempted suicide, but the studio made sure she was treated medically for depression and immediately put back into films. Finally she snapped while making *Annie Get Your Gun* in 1950 and was fired from Metro-Goldwyn-Mayer.

Ironically, this setback forced Garland to undertake a series of concert appearances and tours that revitalized her and her career. In 1954, with her husband, Sid Luft, she produced a spectacular musical remake of *A Star Is Born*. The production was plagued with problems, but under George Cukor's sensitive direction and sensational support from her costar, James Mason, Garland gave her greatest performance on screen, heralded by all as a marvel and justifiably earning her a nomination for the Best Actress Oscar (she lost out to Grace Kelly in *The Country Girl*). Garland was to continue on a bumpy road of lows and highs in her personal and professional life; in 1961 she made yet another legendary comeback at Carnegie Hall, but by the time she died in 1969 at the age of forty-six, her career was over. Nevertheless, her appeal and talent have significantly outshone her tragedy, and today she remains one of show business's twentieth-century icons.

The Wizard of Oz remains a part of American culture in a unique way. It is recognized as one of the glorious achievements of the Golden Age of American filmmaking, and the magic of the production continues to delight audiences around the world to this very day.

THE AMERICAN NEW WAVE—BONNIE AND CLYDE (1967) AND THE GRADUATE (1967)

The shattering aftermath of World War II left the new generation of Europeans disillusioned with the traditional nationalistic values they had fought for. The new dawn and enlightenment had failed to materialize fully in post-war Europe, which left many young people very angry indeed. This anger would eventually translate into new forms of expression, particularly in the arts. Italian filmmakers made "postwar realism" pictures that depicted, in documentary style, the heartbreaks and everyday dangers experienced by the common man. Films such as *The Bicycle Thief* (1948) by Vittorio De Sica, *Open City* (1945) by Roberto Rossellini, and *La Terra Trema* (1948) by Luchino Visconti stunned audiences internationally with their searing portraits of everyday life and tragedy. In the mid-1950s English playwright John Osborne and theater director Tony Richardson would stage a play at the Royal Court Theatre entitled *Look Back in Anger,* featuring the first working-class antihero, Jimmy Porter. Their startling creation ushered in the New Wave of realism, politically and sexually, shaking the foundations of the

British theater. Suddenly Noël Coward was not only out of fashion, he was completely out of touch. Richardson would go on to make films, bringing "the angry young man" to the screen, and along with Karel Reisz and Lindsay Anderson create the British New Wave in films during the end of the fifties and the beginning of the sixties. Such movies as *Saturday Night and Sunday Morning* (1960), *This Sporting Life* (1963), *The Loneliness of the Long Distance Runner* (1962), and *Tom Jones* (1963) made an enormous impact, especially in the art houses of America.

The French followed suit in the 1950s with their "Nouvelle Vague" films of the mid-1950s and 1960s. A group of young film critics, especially influenced by American films of the for-

Mike Nichols's original choice for Benjamin in The Graduate—*Robert Redford.*

ties and fifties, began making movies that were experimental both in the stories they told and in the way the stories were told, using a kind of free-form editing process and a great deal of hand-held camera work. Improvisational techniques became common practice. This young group of critics became France's most prominent filmmakers and chief exponents of the French New Wave, which continues to influence filmmakers to this day. *Breathless* (1959), a film noir masterpiece directed by Jean-Luc Godard from a story by François Truffaut and starring Jean-Paul Belmondo and Jean Seberg, displayed a whole new maturity toward the treatment of sexuality and social isolation as portrayed on screen. *The 400 Blows* (1959), *Shoot the Piano Player* (1960), and *Jules and Jim* (1961)—a trilogy of films by François Truffaut—established a new construct to the way characters dealt with one another. The ménage à trois relationship so brilliantly illuminated in *Jules and Jim* would have a stunning impact on many of the young American intellectuals who flocked to art houses to see it. Directors such as Claude Chabrol, Louis Malle, and Jacques Demy would find a cult following throughout the United States. Two of the young people particularly influenced by the Nouvelle Vague were set designer Robert Benton and magazine journalist David Newman, who had teamed up to write films. Little did they know that the screenplay they had set out to write would pave the way for the American New Wave.

Nearly twenty years had elapsed since the end of World War II before American movies began to experiment with the revolutionary trends already flourishing throughout European cinema. After World War II, Americans were not as disillusioned as the young Europeans had been. The United States emerged as a world power whose own shores had not been devastated by war. Complacent in its conservatism and isolated innocence, America remained for many the land of hope and opportunity. This blind, altruistic spirit dominated the country during the

1950s, but the nation was plunged into darkness when, on a Friday morning in November 1963, President John F. Kennedy was struck down by an assassin's bullet in Dallas, Texas. The president's death, and the subsequent "undeclared" war on North Vietnam by the United States and South Vietnam, would cause a division in this country between young and old, between liberals and conservatives, that would shake the confidence of the American people. In the 1960s, the nation itself would became a battleground of morals. Children questioned their parents' goals and values. Violence erupted on the urban streets of Detroit, Birmingham, New York, and Los Angeles. People started to protest their country's involvement in other nations' affairs. Inevitably a "counterculture" emerged, and with its emergence came the New Wave in American films.

During the 1940s and 1950s, American films saw the decline of the studio system and the rise of international production. Several postwar American films dealt with the social problems of the day. *Gentleman's Agreement* (1947) and *Boomerang* (1947) looked at anti-Semitism. *Home of the Brave* (1949) and *Pinky* (1949) tackled racial problems, and *The Best Years of Our Lives* (1946) explored the difficulties of soldiers returning home after the war. With the exception of the last film, intelligently directed by William Wyler, all the other movies paled beside their European counterparts.

The fifties' films were largely epic in size, with bloated production budgets and locations shot from all over the map. Biblical pictures were popular during this period, as were musicals. Every once in a while an important American film slipped in— *On the Waterfront* (1954), directed by Elia Kazan, or *Paths of Glory* (1957) by Stanley Kubrick—but by the sixties most American films were huge musicals such as *West Side Story* (1961), *Mary Poppins* (1964), and *The Sound of Music* (1965) or

Jane Fonda said no to Bonnie and Clyde *and yes to* Barbarella.

sex comedies like *Lover Come Back* (1961) and *Pillow Talk* (1959) with Doris Day and Rock Hudson. A few brilliant directors did flourish during this period, particularly Alfred Hitchcock, Fred Zinnemann, Billy Wilder, William Wyler, and George Stevens, but their films were exceptions to the rule. No wonder Robert Benton and David Newman looked to the French films of the New Wave for inspiration when they began to write the story of a pair of Depression-era bandits known as Bonnie and Clyde.

Although the legend of Bonnie Parker and Clyde Barrow had provided the material for two previous movies, *They Live by Night* (1947) and *Gun Crazy* (1949)—both film noir classics— Newman and Benton were more influenced by a retrospective of Alfred Hitchcock films at the Museum of Modern Art in 1964 and François Truffaut's *Shoot the Piano Player* and *Jules and Jim.* In fact, they wrote their tale of these attractive misfits with Truffaut in mind to direct.

After completing their first draft, the team managed to capture Truffaut's interest in the project. Truffaut, of course, was familiar with the two previous Bonnie and Clyde–inspired films, and he felt a kinship to the recklessness of the two main characters. He met with the two writers in New York to discuss the project and suggested Benton and Newman go to the actual locales in Texas where Bonnie and Clyde had roamed, then write a better version of their story. They did, but upon their return, they discovered that Truffaut had bowed out in favor of directing a longtime pet project, *Fahrenheit 451,* by Ray Bradbury. He had passed their project on to a fellow director—Jean-Luc Godard. Benton and Newman were thrilled.

The thrill wore off after the team met Godard in New York. The director wanted to do *Bonnie and Clyde,* but he wanted to start shooting in three weeks with a cast of unknowns and shoot it all in France. Benton and Newman said no, and while Godard went back to France to make his science fiction classic *Alphaville,* the script of *Bonnie and Clyde* languished in a drawer. But not for long.

Truffaut had met the young American actor Warren Beatty in Paris while he was living with actress Leslie Caron, who at the time was still married to the English theater director Sir Peter Hall. Truffaut recommended *Bonnie and Clyde* to Beatty, saying he'd be perfect as Clyde Barrow. The next day Beatty called Robert Benton and David Newman, requesting to see the script. Twenty-four hours later he began negotiating with the two writers for an option on the project, intending to produce as well as star in the production. Once Beatty officially owned the project, he approached Arthur Penn, his director on *Mickey One* (1964), with the notion of directing *Bonnie and Clyde*. Penn was a bit reticent at first but ultimately agreed to direct the film if Beatty starred.

The first actress to become interested in playing Bonnie Parker was Leslie Caron, but Beatty knew that a French actress could not possibly play a Texas bank robber. He decided to offer the part to Natalie Wood, his costar in his hit debut film, *Splendor in the Grass* (1961). But Miss Wood wasn't keen on either the script or working with Beatty, who had been a previous lover.

Next Beatty turned to Sue Lyon, who had made a sensational debut in the Stanley Kubrick production of Vladimir Nabokov's immensely infamous novel *Lolita*. Lyon's screen-tested, but the results were not favorable, so Beatty searched on. In a rather odd bit of concept casting, he offered the part to his sister, Shirley MacLaine, but she wisely refused her little brother's offer. Beatty targeted Tuesday Weld and Jane Fonda, but both actresses found the part too immoral and unlikable. Finally, Arthur Penn suggested an actress who had recently received dazzling reviews in an Irish stage play called *Hogan's Goat*. Formerly a top fashion model, she had made a few unsuccessful and unmemorable movies, which meant she could be gotten quite

Warren Beatty originally wanted former girlfriend Natalie Wood for his costar in Bonnie and Clyde.

inexpensively. Her name was Faye Dunaway.

Beatty hated her and fought bitterly with Penn over the notion of casting Dunaway as Bonnie Parker. Finally, though, he agreed to do so, although he remained doggedly skeptical of her ability to realize the character.

The rest of the cast was filled with newcomers from the New York stage. Gene Hackman, who had played opposite Sandy Dennis on Broadway in *Any Wednesday* during the 1964–1965 season, was cast as Clyde's brother, Buck Barrow. Michael J. Pollard, a New York stage actor who'd first come to prominence in the musical *Bye, Bye, Birdie,* was cast as C. W. Moss, a

Tuesday Weld was considered for the role of Bonnie Parker in Bonnie and Clyde.

member of the Barrow gang. Estelle Parsons made her film debut as Buck Barrow's hysterical wife, Blanche. And among the minor players was Gene Wilder as the undertaker.

Filming commenced in Texas in 1966. Little attention was paid to the production by either the press or Warner Bros., who was financing the film for under $2 million. During shooting, Beatty's attitude toward Dunaway changed completely as he saw the way she transformed herself into Bonnie Parker, approaching the part with intelligence and a kind of raw sexuality. She also understood how the film dealt not only with social misfits, but with the very nature of celebrity. That Bonnie and Clyde had been transformed into folk heroes by all the attention lavished on them by the press of their day was significant and telling. The film was completed on schedule and on budget and was ready to be previewed the following April of 1967.

The preview of *Bonnie and Clyde* was held on a Friday night at the Village Theatre in Westwood, California. The house was packed, and when Warren Beatty's name appeared on the screen there was a noticeable murmur throughout the auditorium. For the next twenty minutes the audience was with the picture. It was different in its style, its quick cutting, its sardonic sense of humor, and the chemistry between Dunaway and Beatty was immediately apparent. Then came the first scene of violence. It was so real, so unlike anything ever seen in an American film before, that it shocked the audience. A number of people walked out. As the scenes became more and more violent, the audience grew quieter and quieter. More people walked out. It was clear the film was having a devastating impact on its audience, but was this good or bad?

At the film's conclusion, when Bonnie and Clyde were shot to death in what was at the time the most hideous massacre ever seen in an American film, the preview audience was speechless. No one applauded as the lights came up. No one said a word. Absolutely silent, they filed out past Warren Beatty and all the

Warner Bros. brass. People couldn't speak except for a few out-side, who were outraged by what they had just seen.

Bonnie and Clyde was revolutionary in its approach to charac-ters, its exploration of character motivation, and its explicit handling of sexuality. It demanded that you sympathize, even fall in love, with its two glamorized psychopathic killers, and it made no excuses for their brutal behavior. For some, this was exciting; for others, repulsive. But for the brass at Warner Bros., it was disastrous.

The following day a deal was struck with Beatty and Warn-ers. The studio's basic concern was getting their money out of the film without putting much into distribution. In their opin-ion, why throw good money after bad? Beatty could handle and promote the film as he saw fit, as long as they made back their investment. Beatty had enormous faith in *Bonnie and Clyde* and agreed, as the film's producer, to waive all rights to the film's profits until after it hit a break-even point—in exchange for a huge percentage thereafter. Warner Bros. gladly agreed to his terms, thinking it sheer folly on his part.

The studio released *Bonnie and Clyde* in a limited run in Texas and Kansas and Oklahoma in July of 1967. Critics quickly dis-missed it, and it did almost no business at the box office. Warn-ers was afraid their worst fears were to be realized. Then Beatty pleaded with the studio heads to allow him to take the film, hold off its release in Los Angeles and New York until August, and let him promote the film on his own terms. Warners, thinking it had little to lose, said yes.

Beatty took *Bonnie and Clyde* and screened it personally for every major American critic of importance. Pauline Kael, film critic for *The New Yorker* magazine, was at that period in time the most highly regarded critic in the country. Kael adored *Bonnie and Clyde* and wrote a ten-page review that called it an "Ameri-can masterpiece which bears the influence of the European mas-ters." Other critics fell in behind her, and by the time *Bonnie and Clyde* opened in August in New York and Los Angeles, it was being touted as the greatest American film of the decade.

Then something extraordinary happened: the film caught on like wildfire among the public and quickly became *the* must-see film of the year. *Newsweek* did a cover story on the film, and Faye Dunaway became the actress of the moment. All of the reviews were glorious except for *Time* magazine's and a scathing notice from Bosley Crowther in the *New York Times*. (The elderly film critic's review proved he was dreadfully out of touch. By the end of the year, the *New York Times* had forced Crowther into retirement and replaced him with a liberal female writer named Renata Adler.)

By the end of the fall of 1967, *Bonnie and Clyde* was still playing to sold-out audiences and had already profited the studio beyond its wildest dreams. Warren Beatty was raking in the cash and had become thought of as one of the most highly respected producers in the community. Faye Dunaway was already making her next film, *The Thomas Crown Affair,* costarring Steve McQueen, the biggest male star of the day. The film's musical theme, "Foggie Mountain Breakdown" by Flatt and Scruggs, was the number one best-selling song in the nation. And a major fashion trend had inundated Seventh Avenue: everyone was dressing in the thirties beret look of Bonnie Parker. Many of the film critics had announced the arrival of the American New Wave with *Bonnie and Clyde*. And, in part, this was true.

Bonnie and Clyde was indeed a milestone in the American New Wave, but it wasn't the only film even that year to reflect the tenor of the times. Stanley Kubrick, perhaps the finest American filmmaker of the second half of this century, certainly had been doing his share to transform American films. His black comedy about nuclear war, *Dr. Strangelove or: How I Learned to Stop Worrying and Love the Bomb* (1964), was an innovation in American filmmaking. *Who's Afraid of Virginia Woolf?* (1966) had

revolutionized American film in its depiction of modern rela-
tionships and its use of strong language. *Bonnie and Clyde,* in
every respect, offered a new way of presenting an American
film, borrowing heavily from the French New Wave in its use of
stop motion and jump-cut editing, and in its nonjudgmental
presentation of morally questionable characters.

Finally, one film made during this period spoke to and for an
entire generation, reflecting its time and place more acutely
than any other American film. Today it remains just as insightful
and delightfully anti-Establishment as it did in 1967, when it became one of the pillars of the American New Wave.

The Graduate was based on a novel of the same name by
Charles Webb, published in 1964. In it, Benjamin Braddock, a
returning college graduate from a Gentile family of means in
Pasadena, finds himself unprepared to do anything but surf. He
spends his summer having an affair with Mrs. Robinson, the
wife of his father's business partner. Benjamin becomes in-
fatuated with Mrs. Robinson's daughter, Elaine, much to Mrs.
Robinson's displeasure. When Benjamin tells Elaine about his
shameful affair with her mother, she refuses to see him ever
again. Months pass. Benjamin pursues Elaine up at her college
and finally breaks up her intended marriage to a stuffed shirt.
The two run away from all the hypocrisy and materialistic corruption their parents represent. It's the younger generation telling the older one to "shove it."

A young producer of taste, Larry Turman, optioned the
rights to the book and hired Broadway's hottest new director,
Mike Nichols, to make his feature-film debut as director. Production on *The Graduate* was to start in 1965, but Nichols was
suddenly offered the plum assignment of directing the film version of Edward Albee's monumental play *Who's Afraid of Virginia
Woolf?,* starring Elizabeth Taylor and Richard Burton, so *The
Graduate* was postponed.

Meanwhile Turman began casting the film. Patricia Neal was

signed as Mrs. Robinson, and Warren Beatty was offered the role of Benjamin. Beatty turned down the role, and in the interval between saying yes and actually filming *The Graduate,* Miss Neal suffered a life-threatening stroke that paralyzed her for nearly three years.

After Beatty's rejection, Turman and Nichols decided to offer Benjamin to Robert Redford, whom Nichols had successfully directed in the 1964 play hit *Barefoot in the Park.* Redford agreed to do the part, and although Turman wasn't completely convinced that the actor was right for the role, he began negotiating for Redford's services.

To replace Patricia Neal, Mike Nichols sought out Doris Day, as unlikely a candidate for the seductive Mrs. Robinson as one could imagine. Nevertheless, a script was sent to Miss Day, who was repulsed at what she found and immediately turned down the part.

Turman, meanwhile, was still expressing doubts over Redford, saying he looked too old and too knowing for the part. It was at this point that Nichols agreed and decided to cast Benjamin against type. By making him more ethnic and less like a good-looking blond surfer, Nichols actually broadened the character's appeal. Now Benjamin was like many people his age whose parents had insisted they get a college education—in some cases as a way to avoid Vietnam—only to find themselves unprepared to face the real world once they'd graduated. This gave Benjamin a universal appeal, and his plight brilliantly reflected the mood and attitude of the college generation of the late 1960s.

For the part of Benjamin Braddock, Nichols and Turman cast a relatively unknown stage actor named Dustin Hoffman. Hoffman was thirty years old at the time, nearly ten years too old for the part, but he perfectly encapsulated "the lost college graduate of the new lost generation." For the role of Mrs. Robinson, Anne Bancroft was selected. At the time, Miss Bancroft seemed

Patricia Neal was signed to play Mrs. Robinson, but she suffered a severe stroke before shooting began.

like a peculiar choice for the material. To begin with, although she was portraying a woman old enough to be Benjamin Braddock's mother, Bancroft was just six years older than Dustin Hoffman. She had made a reputation for herself in the Broadway production of *Two for the Seesaw,* playing opposite Henry Fonda under Arthur Penn's direction, then followed this with her electrifying Tony Award–winning performance as Helen Keller's teacher and companion, Anne Sullivan, in *The Miracle Worker.* When she and Patty Duke, as the young Helen, reprised their performances in the 1962 film version, both were honored with

Academy Awards for their work. Two years later, in 1964, Miss Bancroft was once again nominated for Best Actress as the mentally unstable wife and mother in the highly hysterical British-produced melodrama *The Pumpkin Eater*. In fact, the majority of Miss Bancroft's film work was of a highly dramatic nature. She was hardly known for her comedic skills, but Mike Nichols instinctively recognized her potential.

Candice Bergen was first considered for the role of Elaine, Mrs. Robinson's college-age daughter. But Katharine Ross was chosen instead, even though she was unknown at the time. (Ni-

Mike Nichols sought Candice Bergen as Elaine Robinson, but later he used her in Carnal Knowledge.

chols later used Bergen in his 1971 film, *Carnal Knowledge,* and we get a glimpse of what her Elaine Robinson might have been.)

Filming began in March of 1967 and lasted through August of that year. For six weeks prior to actual shooting, Nichols rehearsed his cast as though he were mounting a Broadway production. The time spent working this way contributed greatly to the sensational acting that graces *The Graduate.* The timing between Bancroft and Hoffman is exquisitely droll and very sexy indeed.

The Graduate was booked to open that Christmas, but its distributor, a smaller independent called Avco Embassy, had only managed to obtain bookings in smaller, offbeat theaters in Los Angeles and New York. Moreover, very little publicity had been generated for the film. So early in December, Avco began to have screenings of *The Graduate,* hoping to spur some kind of word-of-mouth buzz. Using the small screening room underneath a bank on Sunset Boulevard, the studio showed the film to anyone they could get inside the theater. And within a day after the first wave of screenings, the word was out that something extraordinary was coming at Christmastime.

The Graduate opened the week of Christmas to the best reviews of the year. Nichols was hailed as the new Preston Sturges. Dustin Hoffman was the talk of the town, as was Anne Bancroft for her searingly funny and sad performance as Mrs. Robinson. Katharine Ross as Elaine was looked upon as a major new discovery. The score by Simon and Garfunkel was one of the first to use rock music. The song "Mrs. Robinson," became the number one best-selling single in the country, and the sound track to the film duplicated its success on the album charts.

The Graduate was a smash hit from the moment of its release, and lines circled around the theater throughout its exclusive engagement. The film had an attitude that wryly expressed the feelings of a younger generation fed up with the plastic and shallow materialistic values of their parents. Clearly, it had its finger on the pulse of an entire generation—which just happened to comprise the vast majority of the moviegoing public—and it communicated its message with a new kind of frankness, a breakthrough approach to erstwhile risqué or tasteless material. The film had shown America its values and mockingly exposed them for the sham they had become.

The Academy of Motion Picture Arts and Sciences nominated both *Bonnie and Clyde* and *The Graduate* as Best Picture of 1967. *Bonnie and Clyde* received ten nominations and *The Graduate* seven, including Best Actor (Dustin Hoffman), Best Actress (Anne Bancroft), and Best Supporting Actress (Katharine Ross), as well as Best Director and Best Screenplay. But on Oscar night *The Graduate* won only one award, for Best Director, while *Bonnie and Clyde* received only two—Best Supporting Actress (Estelle Parsons) and Best Cinematography. The rather pretentious but politically correct film on racism, *In the Heat of the Night,* won Best Picture of 1967.

Today, *Bonnie and Clyde* is still seen as a watershed American film of the sixties and generally considered father of the American New Wave. Warren Beatty has continued to have a success-

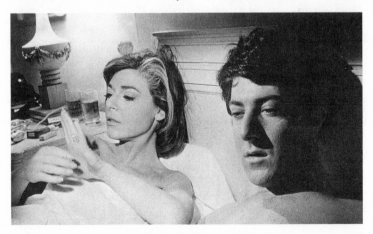

Anne Bancroft and newcomer Dustin Hoffman made film history as the stars of The Graduate, one of the seminal American films of the sixties.

ful career as a producer, actor, writer, and director, with such films as *Shampoo* (1975), *Heaven Can Wait* (1978), *Reds* (for which Beatty was honored with an Oscar as Best Director of 1981), and, most recently, *Dick Tracy* (1990). Faye Dunaway is still active in motion pictures. She was nominated for Best Actress in the Roman Polanski classic thriller *Chinatown* (1974) and won the Oscar for Best Actress in 1976 as the ruthless TV executive in *Network*. Afterward Dunaway's career began to slip, and today she appears in major supporting parts in both television and films. Gene Hackman has rarely stopped working since *Bonnie and Clyde* and remains one of America's finest actors. In 1992 he won the Best Supporting Actor Award for *Unforgiven*.

The Graduate, in retrospect, is just as wonderful today as it was twenty-five years ago. Anne Bancroft is still active in films, television, and stage. Dustin Hoffman is considered one of the best American actors working today. He received two Best Actor Oscars, for *Kramer vs. Kramer* (1979) and *Rain Man* (1988). He was nominated not only for *The Graduate* in 1967, but for *Midnight Cowboy* (1969), *Lenny* (1974), and *Tootsie* (1982). Mike Nichols is still very active and highly regarded. He's made such films as *Catch-22* (1970), *Carnal Knowledge* (1971), *Silkwood* (1983), *Working Girl* (1988), and *Postcards from the Edge* (1991), but he never again attained the icy yet insightful heights of comedy and originality demonstrated in *The Graduate*.

In early 1955 Metro-Goldwyn-Mayer purchased the film rights to Tennessee Williams's Pulitzer Prize–winning play *Cat on a Hot Tin Roof* as a vehicle to star Grace Kelly and James Dean. Six months later Dean was killed in an automobile accident, and the following year Grace Kelly retired from acting to become the princess of Monaco. Elizabeth Taylor and Paul Newman went on to star in the 1958 screen version, which earned both of them Academy Award nominations.

———

The eponymous role in *Dirty Harry* was first offered to John Wayne, who turned it down. Frank Sinatra was next in line, but he too was not inclined to play the San Francisco cop. Paul Newman was offered the part, but after he turned it down as well, Clint Eastwood was approached. Clint said yes—and it made his day and his career by doing so.

———

Stanley Kubrick's first choice for the role of Humbert Humbert in *Lolita* was the urbane Noël Coward. Coward didn't feel people would believe he was really interested in seducing a twelve-year-old girl, so James Mason got the role of his life.

———

Annette Bening was set to play Cat Woman in *Batman Returns* (1992), but she became pregnant with Warren Beatty's child. Michelle Pfeiffer replaced her and had the biggest commercial success of her career.

When Warren Beatty wanted Sue (Lolita) Lyon for Bonnie and Clyde, *her career had already slipped into obscurity.*

———

Tom Selleck was Steven Spielberg's first choice for Indiana Jones, but Selleck was unable to get out of his television series commitment—"Magnum, P.I."—so Harrison Ford was cast instead.

———

Both *American Gigolo* (1980) and *An Officer and a Gentleman* (1982) were developed for John Travolta as star. Travolta got cold feet on both projects at the last moment, so both parts went to Richard Gere, establishing him as a major movie star while Travolta's career slid downhill.

———

Michael Sarrazin was cast as Joe Buck in John Schlesinger's *Midnight Cowboy* (1969), but he turned the part down and opted to do *In Search of Gregory* with Julie Christie. Jon Voight went on to play Joe Buck, for which he received an Oscar nomination as Best Actor.

———

Jack Warner's first choice for the role of Stanley Kowalski in the 1951 film version of *A Streetcar Named Desire* was not its originator, Marlon Brando, but John Garfield. Garfield turned the part down because of bad health, and Brando was hired to repeat his legendary stage performance in the film.

———

Burt Lancaster was set to play the part of the homosexual cellmate, Molina, in *The Kiss of the Spider Woman,* but after suffering a heart attack he found he was no longer insurable. William Hurt eventually played the part in the 1985 film and won an Academy Award as Best Actor of the year.

Alfred Hitchcock was furious when a pregnant Vera Miles had to pull out of *Vertigo* just two weeks before shooting commenced. Kim Novak replaced Miles, and although many have praised Novak's performance, Hitchcock never liked her in the movie and blamed her for the film's initial failure commercially as well as critically. Today, *Vertigo* is considered a masterpiece.

Jennifer Jones waged a heavy campaign for the lead in *Tea and Sympathy* (1956). She was at a Sunday afternoon party at Clifton Webb's home when her agent told her that Deborah Kerr had snagged the coveted role. The normally shy Jones responded by leading a conga line of fully clothed guests into the swimming pool.

Popeye Doyle, the main character in *The French Connection* (1971), was based on a New York cop named Eddie Egan. Egan wanted Rod Taylor or the pudgy Jimmy Breslin to play him in the film. Instead the part went to Gene Hackman, who won an Oscar for Best Actor.

Clark Gable is the only actor to have played a role in one film—*Red Dust* (1932)—and the same role in its remake—*Mogambo*—some twenty years later!

Two weeks into the shooting of *Back to the Future* (1985), Eric Stoltz was fired and replaced by Michael J. Fox. The movie turned Fox into a bankable Hollywood star.

When Howard Hawks remade *The Front Page*, he changed one of the lead characters from a male reporter to a female one and re-titled the picture *His Girl Friday* (1940). Hawks's first choice for Hildy Parks was Jean Arthur, who wasn't interested. Irene Dunne, Claudette Colbert, and Ginger Rogers all said no to Hawks as well. Finally Rosalind Russell was cast opposite Cary Grant, and she gave one of the greatest comedic performances in American film history.

Charles Laughton was set to play the wonderful schoolmaster in *Goodbye, Mr. Chips* (1939), but he pulled out when he decided the part was too treacly. Robert Donat inherited the role and went on to win an Academy Award for Best Actor over Clark Gable in *Gone With the Wind*, James Stewart in *Mr. Smith Goes to Washington*, and Laurence Olivier in *Wuthering Heights*.

Ava Gardner was the studio's first selection to play the fading movie queen Alexandra del Lago in the film version of Tennessee Williams's *Sweet Bird of Youth* (1962). But evidently the role cut too close to home for Miss Gardner's taste, so Geraldine Page, who had created the character on Broadway, was used in the film. Miss Page was nominated for an Oscar for her performance in *Sweet Bird of Youth*.

Michael Curtiz was insistent about using Barbara Stanwyck for the lead in *Mildred Pierce* (1945). But after Stanwyck turned the part down—she'd already done her ''sacrificing mother'' routine in *Stella Dallas* (1937)—the studio forced Joan Crawford on director Curtiz. Curtiz disliked Crawford and bullied her badly on the set. But it was worth it. Joan Crawford won an Oscar for Best Actress as Mildred in *Mildred Pierce.*

When Grace Kelly announced her intention to return to the screen in the 1964 Alfred Hitchcock production of *Marnie,* all of Monaco protested, saying it wasn't dignified. Princess Grace gave in under pressure, and instead Tippi Hedren starred in *Marnie,* receiving heavy criticism for doing a poor imitation of Grace Kelly in the part.

When the Quaker classic *Friendly Persuasion* was originally bought for filming, Frank Capra was set to direct and Bing Crosby and Jean Arthur were announced as the stars. By the time the film finally went into production ten years later, William Wyler was its director, with an uneasy Gary Cooper in the lead.

Although William Holden expressed enormous interest in playing Bick Benedict, the wealthy Texas rancher in George Stevens's outstanding production of Edna Ferber's best-selling generational novel, *Giant,* Stevens stuck by his first choice of Rock Hudson. This shocked the Hollywood establishment at the time, because Holden was considered a much better actor. In addition, Stevens gave Hudson his choice of leading ladies. While Stevens preferred Grace Kelly, Hudson insisted on Elizabeth Taylor. James Dean was cast as the oil baron outsider, Jett Rink, only after Alan Ladd turned down the part. It was Dean's last film.

Dustin Hoffman's estranged wife, Joanna, in *Kramer vs. Kramer* (1979) was to be played by Kate Jackson, who was then starring in a successful TV series, "Charlie's Angels." When Jackson ran into a conflicting availability problem, she was forced to keep her commitment to the TV series. Meryl Streep replaced her and won an Oscar for her performance. Meanwhile Gail Strickland was cast as the lady next door, but Dustin Hoffman was not happy with this choice and made Miss Strickland feel so uncomfortable that she began to stutter from nerves. Hoffman used this ploy to replace her with Jane Alexander, who was later nominated for an Oscar for her performance.

———

Marilyn Monroe desperately wanted to prove herself as a dramatic actress, so she went after the title role in Tennessee Williams's original 1956 script, *Baby Doll*. But director Elia Kazan just couldn't see Monroe in a crib sucking her thumb. He did, however, see British actress Diane Cilento in the role, but oddly enough, she refused it. Carroll Baker was cast and achieved stardom and an Oscar nomination for her performance.

———

Lana Turner quit the Otto Preminger production of *Anatomy of a Murder* (1959), saying her wardrobe wasn't glamorous enough. Lee Remick happily accepted both the role and the wardrobe, and her deliciously sexy performance made her a star.

———

Frank Capra cast Cary Grant in the film version of the hit Broadway comedy *Arsenic and Old Lace* (1944) only after Bob Hope turned it down. Boris Karloff, who had been in the New York production, was unavailable for the film, and Raymond Massey played the part, using makeup to resemble Karloff.

Robert Donat collapsed on the set of *Hobson's Choice* (1954), and David Lean, the director, replaced him with his former *Great Expectations* star John Mills.

Character actor Paul Douglas was perfectly cast as the heel in Billy Wilder's bittersweet comedy *The Apartment* (1960). Unfortunately, Douglas died two weeks before filming began. He was replaced by Fred MacMurray, who had played a louse only once before—in Billy Wilder's film noir classic *Double Indemnity* (1944). These two performances are, without question, MacMurray's best.

Although Vivien Leigh had appeared in the London stage production of Tennessee Williams's *A Streetcar Named Desire,* she was not the original choice for the film version. Olivia De Havilland, fresh from winning her second Academy Award for *The Heiress,* was first choice to play Blanche Du Bois. Miss De Havilland read the script, felt Blanche was too reprehensible to play, and turned down one of the greatest female roles ever written. Miss Leigh was cast instead and won her second Academy Award for her performance in the film.

It was difficult to find strong leading men to play opposite Greta Garbo, since most "Garbo vehicles" left little for a leading man to do but support the star. But when William Powell was set to work with her on *Ninotchka,* it seemed as though Garbo were in luck. Unfortunately Powell bowed out on the assumption that the picture would most likely be no more than a showcase for the actress—just another "Garbo vehicle" where the star laughed for the first time. William Powell was replaced by Melvyn Douglas, who was competent but lackluster in the role.

———

Born on the Fourth of July (1989) changed the course of Tom Cruise's career. His searing portrayal of Vietnam paraplegic vet Ron Kovic won him an Oscar nomination for Best Actor, a Golden Globe Award, and a *Time* magazine cover. Few knew that the film had originally been under consideration ten years before, with Al Pacino slated to play Kovic. When financing fell through, Pacino backed out of the project.

———

Franco Zeffirelli chose to remake *The Champ* for his first American film. Ryan O'Neal was cast to play the part that had originally won Wallace Beery an Academy Award. When O'Neal suggested his son, Griffin, for the other leading role, a screen test was made with O'Neal opposite his son. Zeffirelli wasn't pleased with the test, and when he refused to put Griffin in the film, father Ryan quit the project. Fortunately for Franco, Jon Voight, who had just made a big comeback with his performance in *Coming Home* (1978) was available. By the time *The Champ* was released in April of 1979, Voight had won the Oscar for Best Actor in *Coming Home*.

———

When Burt Reynolds turned down the part of the "astronaut next door" in *Terms of Endearment* (1983) because he felt it was a supporting role, James Brooks was lucky to replace him with Jack Nicholson. Nicholson enjoyed one of his biggest successes in the part and won his second Academy Award for Best Supporting Actor.

———

Ali MacGraw wanted very much to star as Daisy Buchanan in a film of her favorite book, *The Great Gatsby*. Robert Evans, Miss MacGraw's husband at the time and head of production of Paramount Pictures, discussed the project with Frank Yablans, then president of Paramount Pictures, who objected to both MacGraw and the film. But Evans talked Charles Bludhorn, the chairman of the board, into green-lighting the project, with Ali MacGraw, Warren Beatty, and Jack Nicholson envisioned as the three lead characters. But the Evans-MacGraw marriage began to disintegrate, and Ali subsequently decided to make a film with Steve McQueen called *The Getaway* (1972). On the set of that picture, McQueen and MacGraw fell in love. When MacGraw sued Evans for divorce, Paramount decided against casting her as Daisy. Mia Farrow was hired in her place and filmed most of the picture quite pregnant with André Previn's child. Beatty was replaced by Robert Redford, who never felt comfortable in the part, and Bruce Dern substituted for Jack Nicholson. Although the film made money upon its release thanks to a heavy promotional campaign, it was savaged by the critics, and the public didn't much take to it. Ali MacGraw went on to marry Steve McQueen.

———

While Bob Fosse was making his film directorial debut with *Sweet Charity* (1969), starring Shirley MacLaine, he proposed her for the part of Sally Bowles in his upcoming venture, a musical of Christopher Isherwood's *Goodbye to Berlin* known as *Cabaret*. MacLaine was to be part of the *Cabaret* package, but when *Sweet Charity* opened and bombed, she dropped out of the deal. Liza Minnelli replaced her and won the Oscar as the Best Actress of 1972.

———

When Barbra Streisand decided to redo *A Star Is Born* (1976), it was the fourth time the material had been filmed. (It first was seen in 1932 as *What Price Hollywood?* for David O. Selznick. Selznick then remade it five years later as *A Star Is Born* with Janet Gaynor and Fredric March. And it became Judy Garland's comeback musical in 1954, still called *A Star Is Born,* costarring James Mason.) For the leading role of Norman Maine, Streisand wanted Elvis Presley. Presley was more than interested, but after a serious disagreement over billing, he pulled out of the project and Kris Kristofferson took over. The film was a financial hit but a critical dud.

Murder on the Orient Express (1974) marked the return of the "all-star cast," a beautifully realized ensemble of major acting talent, glamorously presented. Dyson Lovell cast the film for producers Richard Goodwin and John Brabourne, who accepted all his original suggestions except one: for the part of the grand duchess, Lovell wanted Marlene Dietrich. The producers felt the idea was too campy and instead went for Wendy Hiller, who gave the hammiest performance in the film.

Reversal of Fortune chronicled attorney Alan Dershowitz's celebrated defense of Claus Von Bulow, played brilliantly by Jeremy Irons. To play the part of Dershowitz, first choice was none other than Woody Allen. Allen didn't pan out, and Ron Silver inherited the role. (Oddly enough, when Mia Farrow became involved in a bitter child custody case with Woody Allen, she used Alan Dershowitz as her attorney.)

Director Ridley Scott claims the two female leads in *Thelma and Louise* were written expressly for Susan Sarandon and Geena Davis, but Meryl Streep and Goldie Hawn had at one point considered doing the roles. Ms. Streep couldn't accept the part because of a previous commitment to Mike Nichols and *Postcards from the Edge* (1991), and Ms. Hawn was talked out of doing the film by her agent, Ron Meyer. Miss Sarandon and Miss Davis went on to play the notorious couple and were rewarded with Oscar nominations for the 1991 hit film.

The scandalous Ken Russell film *Crimes of Passion* (1984), starring Kathleen Turner, was originally slated to have Tom Berenger as its costar. Berenger dropped out of the project after receiving a higher offer from Paramount for *Firstborn,* but an automobile accident prevented the actor from appearing in either film. He was replaced in *Crimes* by John Laughlin.

Norman Jewison's 1987 hit comedy romance, *Moonstruck,* was developed by Sally Field for her own production company. In the end, Miss Field was unhappy with the script and decided against playing the lead role. The part was later played by Cher, who won an Academy Award for her performance.

Timothy Hutton came in to audition for the role of David in Franco Zeffirelli's production of Scott Spencer's novel *Endless Love.* At the time of his reading, Mr. Hutton had not yet been seen in his Academy Award–winning role in *Ordinary People.* For his audition, Mr. Hutton did a scene from his forthcoming film for the producer's assistant, Jeff Burkhart. Mr. Burkhart wrote just two words after Hutton's audition—"Hire him." Mr. Zeffirelli, though, would not consider Mr. Hutton, whom he felt looked too ordinary. Mr. Burkhart and Dyson Lovell, the film's producer, then recommended an unknown actor for the lead named Tom Cruise, but Mr. Zeffirelli passed on Cruise in favor of Martin Hewitt, another unknown found at an open call in Los Angeles. For the part of Jade, the beautiful girl of David's obsession, the producer wanted a young actress he'd found in New York—Sharon Stone. But when Brooke Shields, *the* girl of the moment, was available, executive producers Jon Peters and Peter Guber insisted on Shields for the lead. The film opened in 1981 and was the last successful picture Miss Shields made. Mr. Hewitt seemed overwhelmed by the role, and the critics and public were generally underwhelmed by Mr. Hewitt. Tom Cruise was used in the film in a minor part, although his voice was dubbed by another actor in Los Angeles during postproduction.

———

Steven Spielberg followed his *Jaws* hit with his science fiction classic, *Close Encounters of the Third Kind* (1977). The young director had originally envisioned an older man for the leading role, so he sought out Jack Nicholson. When Nicholson turned down the part to direct his own film, *Goin' South* (1977), Spielberg gave the part to Richard Dreyfuss after the actor had waged a heavy campaign to win the role.

———

Jeff Kanew, who was originally set to direct *Dead Poets Society* (1989), wanted the then unknown actor Liam Neeson for the role of the teacher. Later on Kanew was replaced by Peter Weir, who sought Dustin Hoffman for the part. Hoffman passed, and Robin Williams was cast. Williams received his second Best Actor Oscar nomination for his performance in the 1989 hit.

———

Woody Allen is perhaps the only director to have shot one version of a film and then gone back and shot a second version. Such was the case with his 1987 psychodrama *September*. In the first rendition, the cast included Pulitzer Prize–winning playwright Sam Shepard, Charles Durning, and Maureen O'Sullivan, mother of the film's star, Mia Farrow. The second time around, Shepard, Durning, and O'Sullivan were replaced by Sam Waterston, Denholm Elliott, and Elaine Stritch. The film was a critical and financial failure and remains the worst film ever made by Mr. Allen.

Jacqueline Susann wrote perhaps the best "trash" novel of all time, *Valley of the Dolls,* and its film version was anxiously awaited. The original cast included Natalie Wood, Jane Fonda, Barbara Harris as Neely O'Hara, and Bette Davis as Helen Lawson. By the time filming began, Barbara Parkins and Sharon Tate had replaced Wood and Fonda, and Patty Duke was on board as Neelly O'Hara. Judy Garland was playing Helen Lawson, the queen of Broadway, but after eleven days of shooting Garland was fired (she was said to be uncooperative, and her performance in the rushes was uneven) and replaced by Susan Hayward. The film opened in December of 1967, and although a commercial hit, it was an embarrassment for everyone involved. Barbara Parkins's career fizzled. Sharon Tate was the unfortunate victim of the Charles Manson gang, and Patty Duke never quite recovered from her kitschy performance.

Kirk Douglas had acquired the property *One Flew over the Cuckoo's Nest* and played the lead, Kilroy, in the ill-fated 1964 Broadway production. He tried in vain to make a film version of the material but finally gave up and handed the property to his actor-son, Michael. Michael cast Jack Nicholson in the lead and had Anne Bancroft lined up for the role of Nurse Ratched. Then Bancroft backed out, feeling the role was too black, and Angela Lansbury was set for the part. But Miss Lansbury was playing in *Gypsy* on Broadway at the time and could not break her commitment to the play. Thus the little-known actress Louise Fletcher landed the part and won the 1975 Best Actress Academy Award for her performance in this classic film.

Robert Evans originally wanted Ail MacGraw, then his wife, to star in Roman Polanski's classic thriller *Chinatown* (1974), in the part of Evelyn Mulwray. But when MacGraw ran off with *Getaway* costar Steve McQueen, she ended her marriage and lost the lead in Robert Towne's superb drama. Faye Dunaway, whose career was sagging, replaced MacGraw and was nominated for an Academy Award for her work.

Dustin Hoffman desperately wanted Goldie Hawn to play opposite him in his comedy classic *Tootsie* (1982), but Ms. Hawn felt the gender-bender film was too much Hoffman's vehicle. Jessica Lange was cast instead and brought a sadness to the part that wasn't in the script. Ms. Lange had just finished her soul-wrenching performance as Frances Farmer in *Frances* when she began filming *Tootsie,* and she felt she brought a lot of Frances to her *Tootsie* performance. Mr. Hoffman wasn't particularly pleased with Miss Lange's interpretation, but everyone else was. She won Best Supporting Actress Oscar for her stunning work in *Tootsie* and was also established as one of Hollywood's finest actresses.

The all-star *Murder on the Orient Express* success spawned a series of Agatha Christie all-star mysteries. *The Mirror Crack'd* (1980) was third in the series. Natalie Wood was set to star as the aging actress, but when she got into a major argument with Guy Hamilton, the film's director, she quit the film and was replaced by Elizabeth Taylor, who at the time was married to Senator John Warner. The film was poorly directed by Mr. Hamilton, but the experience prompted Miss Taylor to try playing Broadway, where she triumphantly appeared in the 1981 revival of Lillian Hellman's classic *The Little Foxes*.

In 1939 Columbia Pictures bought the rights to C. S. Forester's adventure novel *The African Queen,* with Charles Laughton and his wife, Elsa Lanchester, in mind for the leads. When this did not pan out, Columbia sold the rights to Warner Bros., who saw *The African Queen* as a perfect vehicle for Bette Davis, then the reigning star of the lot, and David Niven. Finally John Huston acquired the rights and cast his old friend Humphrey Bogart and the wonderful Katharine Hepburn in his flawless 1951 production. Hepburn was nominated for an Oscar for her performance, and Bogart won the Academy Award as Best Actor.

Michael Caine had already made two impressive films, *The Ipcress File* (1965) and *Zulu* (1964), when he reached international prominence for his brilliant work as the roguish Cockney cad in *Alfie* (1966). Based on the English hit play, *Alfie* was forever to be associated with Caine, but Lewis Gilbert, the film's director, had not originally considered him for the part. Prior to Caine, Gilbert had sought unsuccessfully to interest Terence Stamp, Anthony Newley, and Laurence Harvey in the role. Fortunately for us and Caine, they all turned it down.

———

When Columbia Pictures bought the rights to Truman Capote's nonfiction novel *In Cold Blood,* they were worried that the downbeat subject matter—the killing of a Kansas family by two psychopaths—was not box office material. They felt the celebrated book needed star power to insure its success. Thus, for the leading roles of the two killers, the studio wanted Paul Newman and Steve McQueen. The film's producer/writer/director, Richard Brooks, and the book's author, Truman Capote, were horrified at this notion and insisted against casting stars in the roles. Brooks and Capote won out, and Robert Blake and Scott Wilson were cast for the leads. Blake's performance was superb, and the film was well received critically, but Columbia had been correct in one respect: the subject matter was uncommercial. *In Cold Blood* (1967) was not a box office success.

———

Frank Capra was one of Hollywood's best directors, but he hadn't quite hit his stride until he directed his 1934 screwball comedy classic *It Happened One Night.* Originally Capra had gone after the services of Robert Montgomery for the lead as the out-of-work newspaperman. But Montgomery didn't think the script was any good. Capra next went for Clark Gable, whom Metro-Goldwyn-Mayer lent out to Columbia as a kind of punishment for their star's bad behavior. Gable was outraged, particularly since he was not impressed with the script or Mr. Capra. For the part of the runaway heiress, Capra went after Myrna Loy, Miriam Hopkins, Constance Bennett, and Margaret Sullavan. All turned the part down. Finally Capra petitioned Paramount for Claudette Colbert, who was under contract to the studio. Paramount agreed to the loanout, but not before

Miss Colbert bitched about doing the part. All through the shooting of the picture, both stars complained bitterly about their characters, thinking the film inconsequential and dumb. It became the biggest hit of 1934, won Oscars for both Gable and Colbert, as well as Academy Awards for Best Picture, Best Director, and Best Screenplay. (One interesting footnote: *It Happened One Night* was Adolf Hitler's favorite movie.)

———

Very few films have been as dominated by one performance as *Last Tango in Paris* (1973). Marlon Brando virtually held the film together. Indeed, the movie may be Brando's crowning achievement, and it's difficult to imagine anyone else in the part of the expatriate Paul. But when director Bernardo Bertolucci first decided to make *Last Tango,* he had wanted to use his stars from his previous film, *The Conformist* (1970)—French actor Jean-Louis Trintignant and French actress Dominique Sanda. Sanda was having an affair with Trintignant at the time, but she was also having a battle with drugs. Sanda was not well enough to play the part, and Trintignant was passed over when Brando expressed interest in doing a film with Bertolucci. Brando wound up writing all his own dialogue, uncredited, and he was nominated for his seventh Academy Award for his performance.

———

Robert Redford made his directorial debut with his film adaptation of Judith Guest's novel *Ordinary People* (1980). To play the role of the cold mother, Redford wanted Ann-Margret, who seemed interested and agreed to do the part. Ultimately, however—and unfortunately for her—she was filled with doubts about the unsympathetic part and finally passed. Redford cast television comedy queen Mary Tyler Moore in the part, and she astounded critics and audiences with her magnificent performance. Miss Moore was nominated for an Academy Award, and many felt she was overlooked when she failed to win.

————

Debra Winger was one of the most sought-after actresses after receiving two Oscar nominations for her performances in the hugely successful films *An Officer and a Gentleman* (1982) and *Terms of Endearment* (1983). James Brooks, one of television's brightest talents and director of *Terms of Endearment,* was following up his first film with a scathing satire on network news called *Broadcast News* (1987). Naturally Brooks cast Winger in the lead role, but she had to bow out when she became pregnant by Timothy Hutton, her husband at the time. Holly Hunter, a virtually unknown actress, won the coveted part. Miss Hunter went on to win the New York Film Critics Award for Best Actress for *Broadcast News* and was nominated for an Academy Award.

————

Robert Redford was originally set to play the down-and-out attorney in *The Verdict* (1982) but pulled out of the project because he felt the main character was too seedy. Paul Newman replaced Redford and gave one of the best performances of his career. Newman was nominated for Best Actor for his work in *The Verdict.*

————

Audrey Hepburn was George Stevens's first choice for the wonderful title role in *The Diary of Anne Frank* (1959). Miss Hepburn was approached and an offer was made, but after some consideration Miss Hepburn declined, feeling she just couldn't be convincing as a thirteen-year-old Jewish girl. Stevens went on to cast Millie Perkins, an unknown, in the role. Miss Perkins was severely criticized for her performance upon the film's release, although it may be argued that she's actually quite effective. Miss Perkins's film career was rather limited, and today she is occasionally seen in supporting roles.

After making *This Property Is Condemned* (1966), Natalie Wood decided to take some time off from films. During this period she was offered the leads in *Rosemary's Baby, Bonnie and Clyde,* and *The Diary of a Mad Housewife.* She turned down all three parts and finally returned to the screen in *Bob & Carol & Ted & Alice* (1969).

Carlo Ponti had envisioned his wife, Sophia Loren, as the star of his production of Boris Pasternak's Nobel Prize–winning novel, *Doctor Zhivago* (1965). But since the character of Lara had to age from sixteen to twenty-eight, director David Lean felt Miss Loren might be too old for the part, not to mention too Italian. Mr. Lean and Mr. Ponti squabbled over Miss Loren for several months, but finally the brilliant director won out. He chose to cast the relatively unknown British actress, Julie Christie, and her performance as Lara in *Doctor Zhivago* greatly helped the film's substantial popularity and made Miss Christie an international star.

Bob Fosse's autobiographical musical, *All That Jazz,* was to have starred Paul Newman as the egomaniacal Broadway director. Newman felt uncomfortable with the idea of playing Fosse since he was not a particularly good dancer. Fosse went for Richard Dreyfuss, who had just won an Academy Award for *The Goodbye Girl* (1977). Dreyfuss was set for the role, but one week prior to actual shooting he quit the production, and Roy Scheider stepped in. Scheider received his best reviews and was nominated for an Oscar when the film was released in December of 1979.

————

Pat Conroy's best-selling novel *The Prince of Tides* was originally optioned by actor-director Robert Redford. Redford expressed a deep interest in playing the lead role, but he was unable to come up with a satisfactory screen adaptation. *The Prince of Tides* was eventually directed by Barbra Streisand in 1991, with Nick Nolte in the lead. Nolte won a Golden Globe Award for his performance and was nominated for an Oscar for Best Actor.

————

Mia Farrow was set to star in Woody Allen's 1993 film *Manhattan Murder Mystery* when the papers exploded with the horrific details of her breakup with the neurotic director. Miss Farrow was immediately replaced in Allen's film by former girlfriend Diane Keaton.

————

Judy Garland had recorded all the songs and had filmed several scenes in the film version of Irving Berlin's smash Broadway musical *Annie Get Your Gun* when the studio fired her for her erratic behavior. Garland was replaced by Betty Hutton, and the 1950 film was a smash at the box office upon its release.

————

After Noël Coward turned him down, Stanley Kubrick offered Cary Grant the role of Humbert Humbert in the screen version of *Lolita* (1962). After reading the script, Grant was appalled, and he too declined. Hayley Mills was offered the title role, but her parents felt the character of Lolita was too incongruous to the image Walt Disney had created for her. Unknown Sue Lyon was cast instead.

———

John Huston originally wanted actress Lola Albright for his film noir classic *The Asphalt Jungle* (1950). When Miss Albright was unavailable for the part, he used the little-known Marilyn Monroe instead. Monroe was memorable in the role, and her performance in the film helped establish her as a star.

———

Both Jack Nicholson and Sylvester Stallone turned down the part of the paraplegic Vietnam vet in *Coming Home* (1978). Jon Voight, who had originally been set to play Jane Fonda's husband in the film, took over the part as her lover, and Bruce Dern replaced Voight. Voight won the Academy Award for Best Actor for his work in *Coming Home,* and Bruce Dern received an Oscar nomination for Best Supporting Actor.

———

Anne Baxter finally hit her mark as an actress playing the alcoholic slut in the screen version of W. Somerset Maugham's bestselling novel *The Razor's Edge* (1946). As Sophie, Miss Baxter won the Oscar for Best Supporting Actress. But she was hardly the first choice for the part. Miss Baxter was cast only after Alice Faye, Susan Hayward, Bonita Granville, and Maureen O'Hara had passed on the part.

———

Michelangelo Antonioni's psychological thriller *Blowup* (1966) was one of the seminal works of the 1960s. Terence Stamp was originally sought to play the part of the hip photographer based on real-life David Bailey. But when the Italian film director spotted David Hemmings at a party, he knew at once this was the actor for the part. Hemmings got the role, and the film made him a star.

Kirk Douglas turned down the dual role in the western comedy *Cat Ballou* (1965), and the part went to Lee Marvin instead. Marvin won the Oscar for Best Actor for his comic turn in the film.

Sam Spiegel, producer extraordinaire, was dead set on using his pal Humphrey Bogart for the part of the deranged Colonel Bogie in his lavish screen version of Pierre Boulle's novel *The Bridge on the River Kwai* (1957). Bogart was too ill to play the part, so Spiegel approached Sir Laurence Olivier. Olivier was too involved with his own production of *The Prince and the Show-girl* (1957), costarring Marilyn Monroe, so he too declined. Meanwhile, director David Lean offered the Colonel Bogie role to his mentor, Noël Coward, but Coward didn't want to be on location for such a long time, so he passed. Lean next sought out Charles Laughton for the part. Laughton agreed, but ill health forced him out as well. Finally Alec Guinness was cast in the part and would go on to win both the New York Film Critics Award and the Academy Award for his interpretation of Colonel Bogie. Sam Spiegel offered Cary Grant the part eventually played by William Holden. Grant later said he deeply regretted his decision not to accept Spiegel's offer. Holden made the film under his old contract for Columbia, but rather than receiving his usual salary, he took a percentage of the film's profits. *River Kwai* proved to be an international smash, and Holden made more money on this film than any other during his career.

Joan Fontaine achieved stardom in Alfred Hitchcock's first American film, *Rebecca* (1940), produced by David O. Selznick and based on Daphne du Maurier's best-selling novel. But she had won the role by a narrow margin over Anne Baxter. Moreover, Vivien Leigh had also been anxious to secure the part, particularly since her husband, Laurence Olivier, had been approached to play the male lead after Ronald Colman turned it down. Leigh tested, but it was obvious she was too strong a personality for such a mousy character. Thus, in the end Fontaine was offered the role and perfectly captured the character's charmingly shy qualities.

––––––––

Kim Stanley made a sensation on Broadway when she played Cherie in William Inge's comedy *Bus Stop*. Miss Stanley actively campaigned for the part in the screen version, but instead director Josh Logan selected Marilyn Monroe, who gave one of her best performances in the film. Then, two years later in 1958, Miss Stanley gave a magnificent performance in Paddy Chayefsky's *The Goddess,* playing an unstable actress based heavily on Marilyn Monroe.

––––––––

Howard Hawks wanted Gary Cooper to star in his classic western *Red River,* but Coop wasn't interested. He felt the movie belonged to the role young Monty Clift was playing. Hawks gave the part to John Wayne, who felt it was the finest acting he had done in his career. Cary Grant was approached for a role in the film, but he too said no, and John Ireland was cast instead. Actress Joanne Dru replaced a pregnant Margaret Sheridan.

––––––––

When Robert Donat fell ill just before production began on *Captain Blood* (1935), French actress Lily Damita went to Jack Warner and pleaded to have her husband, Errol Flynn, replace Donat in the title role. Flynn was an unknown actor at the time, but Warner finally gave in and cast Flynn and a young Olivia De

Havilland in the swashbuckler. The movie proved to be a tremendous hit for the studio and instantly made a matinee idol out
of Errol Flynn.

––––––––

Whoopi Goldberg was not a recognizable figure to the
moviegoing public when Steven Spielberg cast her as Celie in his
screen adaptation of Alice Walker's Pulitzer Prize–winning
novel, *The Color Purple*. But this did not stop Ms. Goldberg from
suggesting Tina Turner for the part of Shug, the blues singer and
Celie's lover. Turner was approached, but she felt the role
struck "too close to home." Margaret Avery was cast instead
and was later nominated for an Academy Award as Best Supporting Actress of the year.

––––––––

Roman Polanski was set to make his first American film, *Rose-*
mary's Baby, a sensational thriller written by Ira Levin. For the
terrific part of Rosemary, Polanski wanted to use his wife,
Sharon Tate, but the studio felt she wasn't a strong enough actress for the part. Natalie Wood, Jane Fonda, and Tuesday
Weld were all considered, but finally Mia Farrow, a young TV
actress who had won acclaim on the series "Peyton Place" and
had made headlines when she'd married crooner Frank Sinatra,
was cast as Rosemary. For the part of her husband, Polanski
considered both Robert Redford and Warren Beatty. Jack Nicholson and Laurence Harvey had made it known they were interested in the part of Guy, but finally Polanski settled on John
Cassavetes. (Polanski later said he regretted this decision.) *Rose-*
mary's Baby was a smash hit upon its release in 1968, and it made
a star out of Mia Farrow and won a Best Supporting Actress
Oscar for Ruth Gordon.

––––––––

Steve McQueen wanted to play the Sundance Kid in *Butch Cassidy and the Sundance Kid* (1969), but the studio had wanted Warren Beatty for the part. When McQueen proved to be too particular about the script and his billing, Paul Newman, set to play Butch Cassidy, used his considerable clout to secure Robert Redford as his costar, although he had never met Redford before. The film proved to be an enormous success, Robert Redford suddenly became the hottest male star around, and Paul Newman had another huge hit on his hands.

————

Dino De Laurentiis announced Robert Altman as the director of E. L. Doctorow's best-selling novel *Ragtime*. O. J. Simpson desperately wanted the part of Coalhouse Walker, but Howard E. Rollins was cast instead. Rollins was later to receive an Oscar nomination for his performance. George C. Scott made it clear he wanted to play the father, but James Olson was cast. Suddenly De Laurentiis fired Robert Altman and replaced him with Milos Forman. *Ragtime* was one of 1981's biggest disappointments and a pale imitation of the magnificent book that was its inspiration.

————

The first screen version of Ernest Hemingway's classic novel *A Farewell to Arms* (1932) was to have starred Fredric March and Claudette Colbert. They were replaced by Gary Cooper and Helen Hayes, who emerged as one of the screen's great romantic pairings.

————

Warren Beatty remade the 1941 comedy classic *Here Comes Mr. Jordan* and called it *Heaven Can Wait* (1978). For the part of the angel, Mr. Jordan, wonderfully played in the original by

Claude Rains, Beatty sought out both Cary Grant, who was in retirement, and Senator Eugene McCarthy. Eventually Beatty settled on James Mason, who proved to be something of a disappointment.

Glenn Close achieved stardom when she played the villainous lead in Adrian Lyne's 1986 thriller, *Fatal Attraction*. Close, previously associated with "good girl" roles—such as those in *The World According to Garp* (1982) and *The Natural* (1984)—was chosen only after Debra Winger and Barbara Hershey turned down the role. Miss Close received her third Oscar nomination for the part, and the film established her as a major film star.

When King Vidor was set to make the film version of Ayn Rand's monumental novel, *The Fountainhead* (1949), he envisioned Humphrey Bogart or James Cagney in the role of the determined architect, based loosely on Frank Lloyd Wright. But neither actor cottoned to the part, and Gary Cooper was cast instead. Barbara Stanwyck went after the female lead with a vengeance, and when the studio bypassed her, Stanwyck tore up her studio contract in spite. Ayn Rand suggested Greta Garbo for the part, but Garbo was already in retirement and sent back the script unopened. Ultimately a young Broadway actress, Patricia Neal, was cast in the part. Miss Neal and Mr. Cooper became romantically involved during the filming of *The Fountainhead*, but none of their off-camera heat communicated on screen, and the film was considered an interesting failure. Cooper and Neal continued their affair for several years, although Coop was still very much married.

Yul Brynner originally wanted to direct the film version of Rodgers & Hammerstein's musical smash *The King and I* (1956), and he saw Marlon Brando in the lead. Brando was offered the part but turned it down, so Brynner decided to perform the role himself, elaborating on his Broadway interpretation. Dinah Shore waged a heavy campaign for the role of Anna, but the studio fought her off with force. Vivien Leigh was offered the part, but she suffered still another of her many nervous breakdowns and was uninsurable. Deborah Kerr was an ideal casting choice, even though Marni Nixon had to do all of her singing. Miss Kerr received an Oscar nomination for her performance, and Mr. Brynner won the Oscar for his embellished version of the king of Siam.

In 1983 Paramount Pictures agreed to make Martin Scorsese's highly controversial screen version of Kazantzakis's *The Last Temptation of Christ,* with Aidan Quinn playing Jesus. But at the last minute the studio pulled its financing, and the production was shelved. Five years later Universal Pictures agreed to make the film for a budget of less than $7 million. Scorsese said yes, but this time he chose Willem Dafoe for the part of Jesus. He also replaced rock star Sting in the part of Pontius Pilate with rock star David Bowie. When the movie opened in 1988 it caused a sensation, but it never really developed an audience and remained a box office failure.

For his directing debut, John Huston decided on a third film version of *The Maltese Falcon* (1941). John, son of actor Walter Huston, was at the time one of Hollywood's finest screenwriters. Still, George Raft was not impressed by Huston, so he turned down the part of Sam Spade. Humphrey Bogart, a contract player at Warners, got the part instead. Geraldine Fitzgerald, fresh out of *Wuthering Heights,* found the female lead "vile," so the part went to Mary Astor. *The Maltese Falcon* was a big hit upon its initial release and quickly put Bogart in the forefront of American actors.

When 20th Century–Fox decided to make the screen version of the 1964 smash musical, *Hello, Dolly,* based on Thornton Wilder's comedy *The Matchmaker,* most people thought Carol Channing would reprise her stage performance. At first the studio wanted Channing, then decided she wasn't well known enough. Elizabeth Taylor was considered for the part of Dolly Levi, but she said no. Julie Andrews turned the part down next, and finally the studio settled on Barbra Streisand, fresh from her success in the film version of *Funny Girl* (1969). Ms. Streisand was much too young for the part, and although she tried valiantly to play the role, it just didn't work. *Hello, Dolly* was one of the studio's biggest turkeys.

In 1935 Metro-Goldwyn-Mayer decided to make *Mutiny on the Bounty,* casting their number one male star, Clark Gable, in the role of the courageous Fletcher Christian. Gable hated the part. For the role of the hateful Captain Bligh, the studio first went to Wallace Beery, but Beery arrogantly refused the part. Chares Laughton was cast instead, and film history was made. Franchot Tone was set to play Byam, but only after Robert Montgomery turned the part down. All three actors, Gable, Laughton, and Tone, were nominated for their performances in *Mutiny on the Bounty.*

Frank Sinatra had triumphantly returned to the screen with his Oscar-winning performance in *From Here to Eternity* (1953). Thus it was natural that producer Sam Spiegel would hire him for the lead in his next film, *On the Waterfront* (1954), which was written by Budd Schulberg and to be directed by Elia Kazan. But when Marlon Brando showed interest in the part of Terry Malloy, Kazan pressured Spiegel into firing Sinatra. Sinatra was so angered by this that he actually tried to sue Spiegel for breach of contract. Brando went on to play the part and win an Oscar. Grace Kelly turned down the part of the girlfriend in order to make *Rear Window* for Alfred Hitchcock. Newcomer Eva Marie Saint was cast, and her performance won her the Academy Award for Best Supporting Actress.

George C. Scott reached the pinnacle of his career with his monumental performance in *Patton* (1970). But Scott received the role of the cantankerous World War II general only after Burt Lancaster, Rod Steiger, Robert Mitchum, and Lee Marvin had said no. John Wayne desperately wanted to play the part, but the producers felt he wasn't a good enough actor for the role. Scott won the Oscar for Best Actor that year for his performance, but he refused to accept the award.

Peter Sellers made a career playing the bumbling detective Inspector Clouseau in the Pink Panther series of films. But Sellers, first seen in the part in *The Pink Panther* (1964), was selected for the role he would forever after be identified with only after Peter Ustinov said "No way." And although Ava Gardner was pursued to play the inspector's wife in *The Pink Panther,* she thought the role too dumb. Blake Edwards, the film's director, used Capucine instead.

———

John Huston had wanted to make a film version of Rudyard Kipling's *The Man Who Would Be King* for nearly three decades. This wonderful adventure story had first materialized as a Huston project in the 1950s. Clark Gable and Humphrey Bogart were set to star. Gable backed out after Bogart died, and the project went into limbo. In the early 1970s Huston tried to revive it once more, and Paul Newman and Robert Redford were said to be starring. But the actors didn't care for the script. Finally, in 1975, Huston secured the necessary financing, and he cast Sean Connery and Michael Caine in *The Man Who Would Be King*. When the film opened in late 1975, it was well received critically, but it never found an audience. Today it's considered one of Huston's finest achievements, in no small part due to the wonderful teaming of Connery and Caine.

———

George Lucas, fresh from his hit 1973 film, *American Graffiti*, found it difficult to interest anyone in his next project. Studio after studio turned down his ambitious science fiction fantasy, but finally 20th Century–Fox agreed to make the epic—for a price. Thus *Star Wars* (1977) went into production. Lucas cast an unknown, Mark Hamill, in the lead, but for the part of Han Solo, he selected Harrison Ford, a former carpenter turned actor. Ford got the part only after Lucas rejected both Nick Nolte and Christopher Walken. *Star Wars* was the most successful film of the 1970s, and it made Harrison Ford a leading man.

———

When Alan J. Pakula agreed to write and direct William Styron's powerful best-selling novel, *Sophie's Choice* (1982), he had only one actress in mind—Liv Ullmann. Meanwhile, author

Styron claimed he had imagined Ursula Andress in the part while writing the book. Marthe Keller and Barbra Streisand both tried to win the role, but it finally went to Meryl Streep, who had won an Oscar for her performance in *Kramer vs. Kramer* (1979) and had won an Oscar nomination for her complex performance in *The French Lieutenant's Woman* (1981). Nothing, though, had prepared audiences for her devastating turn as Sophie, and Streep was honored with every award imaginable, including the Oscar for Best Actress.

––––––

When Josh Logan decided to make the film version of the hit Rodgers & Hammerstein musical *South Pacific* (1958), his first choice for Nellie Forbush, the nurse, made memorable on stage by Mary Martin, was none other than the nonsinging Elizabeth Taylor. Taylor was interested in doing the part, but her inability to sing forced her to say no. Doris Day was considered, but after she refused to do an impromptu singing audition for Richard Rodgers at a dinner party, Day was never seriously considered again. The part eventually went to Mitzi Gaynor, who was merely adequate.

––––––

Barbra Streisand had developed the project *The Way We Were* with Arthur Laurents writing the original screenplay. Streisand said no to Ken Howard, who wanted to play Hubbell, her husband. Warren Beatty said no to Ray Stark, the film's producer. Finally Streisand insisted on Robert Redford, who said yes. Their teaming was one of the highlights of the 1973 moviegoing season.

––––––

Ben Kingsley won stardom, universal acclaim, and an Academy Award for his performance in *Gandhi* (1982), the award-winning biography by Sir Richard Attenborough. But Kingsley was hardly the first choice for the part. He was selected only after Dirk Bogarde, Peter Finch, Anthony Hopkins, Albert Finney, Alec Guinness, and Tom Courtney said no.

———

Jack Nicholson had made a number of "B" films before he attained critical and public acclaim as the liberal lawyer in Dennis Hopper's counterculture classic, *Easy Rider* (1969). But Nicholson nearly didn't play the part. Rip Torn was first set in the role, but he quit the production after having a terrific fight with Hopper over the way the character was written. Bruce Dern was then offered the role, but he turned it down. Nicholson was a cool third choice, and his performance in the film made him a star. Nicholson received his first of ten Academy Award nominations for *Easy Rider.*

———

Peter Finch's last performance was his best, as the insane newscaster Howard Beale in Paddy Chayefsky's stinging satire *Network* (1976). But Finch's costar in the film, William Holden, had originally been asked to play Beale; instead, Holden had favored the other male lead. After Holden said no to Beale, director Sidney Lumet offered the part to George C. Scott, Henry Fonda, and Glenn Ford. All echoed Holden's response, and finally Finch was approached with the part. Finch immediately said yes. Both Finch and Holden were nominated for their performances in *Network,* as was Faye Dunaway. Finch died of a heart attack before the Oscar ceremonies, so the award was offered posthumously. Faye Dunaway also won for her work as Diana, and Beatrice Straight was given the Best Supporting Actress award for portraying a character who was only on screen for six minutes.

———

Marilyn Monroe, Tony Curtis, and Jack Lemmon all had creative career milestones when they starred in Billy Wilder's *Some Like It Hot* (1959). But when Wilder originally began casting, he envisioned quite a different trio of players. He wanted Bob Hope and Danny Kaye to play the two musicians on the run in drag and Mitzi Gaynor to play the band singer, Sugar, the part for which Ms. Monroe is best remembered. For whatever reason, Ms. Gaynor declined the role, and her loss became screen history's gain.